SMART MONEY,
DUMB MONEY

**Beating the Crowd
Through Contrarian Investing**

Keith G. Richards, CMT, CIM, FCSI

Praise for Keith's new book!

"If the markets fill you with unease but you aren't sure why, let Keith's third book shape your discontent. *Smart Money, Dumb Money* walks readers through widely followed, well-established technical tools for contrarian investors along with more modern indicators such as Google Trends and social media so they can independently weigh risk and set trading rules. Above all, he reminds us that prioritizing those rules over emotional reactions separate the savvy contrarians from those who are simply contrary. Follow Keith's principles to build confidence in your own path."

— **Robin Poon, Editor of Investor's Digest of Canada**

"Keith is truly contrarian. It is the way he thinks, challenging all assumptions and taking nothing for granted. He is not willing to hide behind an index hugging strategy and is always looking for an edge to stay one step ahead of the markets. Keith uses a variety of different contrarian signals in order to establish the pulse of the market and the highest probability path for different investments. *Smart Money, Dumb Money* reveals Keith's easy-to-use contrarian strategies to help you stay one step ahead of the markets."

— **Brooke Thackray, Research Analyst for Horizons ETF's,**
Author, President of Alpha Mountain Investments

"*Smart Money Dumb Money* is a must-read for every investor seeking to understand contrarian investing and market sentiment. Keith outlines the necessary strategies for readers and their investment tool box."

— **Lana Sanichar, Editor-in-Chief of *Canadian MoneySaver Magazine***

"There's a time to buy and a time to sell and contrarian investing flashes the signals to make the right moves. Listen to the herd or conventional wisdom and you'll see that contrarian investing gets no respect. This excellent book debunks that belief and demonstrates how applying the principles of contrarian investing can work for you. It's a must read for successful investing."

— **Stephen Bernhut, Editor of the *The Money Letter***

"An exceptional book! A fascinating reading into the world of the best kept secrets of the investment industry. Keith Richards has a talent of explaining it all in a way that everyone can understand. This book could have saved investors from painful market crashes, and especially the one of 2008. Read this book. It's going to be the best investment you made this year."

— **Gabriella Szasz, Montreal Chapter Head of the**
Canadian Society of Technical Analysts

SMART MONEY, DUMB MONEY

Beating the
Crowd Through
Contrarian Investing

Keith G. Richards, CMT

Contents

Published in 2021 by
Kinetics Design, KDbooks.ca
ISBN 978-1-988360-62-1 (paperback)
ISBN 978-1-988360-63-8 (ebook)

Cover and interior design, typesetting,
online publishing and printing by Daniel Crack, Kinetics Design,
KDbooks.ca, linkedin.com/in/kdbooks/

Cover photographs by Jessica Rosati, Jessica Rosati Photography
https://www.instagram.com/jessicarosatiphotography/?hl=en

Acknowledgements

I would like to highlight a few of the more influential analysts and writers whom I have drawn knowledge and inspiration from over more than 30 years of financial analysis and contrarian investing.

My original formal teachers of Technical Analysis include Ralph Acampora. Also, the good people involved in the Canadian Society of Technical Analysts along with the New York based Market Technicians Association (MTA) were paramount in my early studies. It was in my effort to obtain the CMT (Chartered Market Technician) designation in the late 1990s that I began studying contrarian investing. In fact, my research paper submitted to the MTA as the final requirement towards the designation highlighted the use of combining a contrarian indicator (the Put-to-Call Ratio), with a traditional Technical Analysis momentum tool (RSI).

The work of Jason Goepfert of SentimentTrader, Larry McDonald of BearTraps, and Brooke Thackray of Alpha Mountain Investments were invaluable in producing this book. Their leadership in the fields of sentiment indicators, capitulation modelling and seasonality work has profoundly influenced my professional work as a Portfolio Manager. I'm grateful that all three of these experts took the time out of their busy schedules to provide insightful interviews for this book. These three brilliant minds represent the pinnacle of "Smart Money" when it comes to the pragmatic use of contrarian trading methodologies.

I would also like to acknowledge the work of my business associate Craig Aucoin, CFA and Portfolio Manager at ValueTrend Wealth Management. Craig is a meticulous and insightful fundamental research analyst whom I both rely on, and learn from. Craig often questions my reasoning and structure behind a technical observation, sometimes forcing me to re-evaluate decisions. Trust me when I say that this type of pushback can only enhance one's discipline as an investor. Craig offered several insights to the production of this book as I researched the Alternative Data space.

Although I am known as the founder of my company, my assistant,

Cindy McIntyre, was the first official employee at ValueTrend Wealth Management (its a long story!). Cindy is my right-hand woman, my organizer, and my friend of 25 years. I owe Cindy so much in the success of my career. Through thick and thin, good times and bad, Cindy has always had my back!

I'd also like to thank Grant Neuber, my friend who I met during my days of working with CIBC Gundy in the early 2000's. Grant has had a distinguished career as Vice President, Branch Manager, and Investment Advisor at Wood Gundy. He has always been in my corner. He is the guy whom I bounce my ambitious projects off of, like this book. He always provides feedback forcing me to think a little deeper about my proposed projects. Grant is no ordinary Investment Advisor. He is a natural leader and a man of great wisdom. Never discouraging, Grant is my "atta boy" coach. But he's not afraid of questioning my decisions.

Last but absolutely not least, I owe my wife, Jane Richards, the biggest debt of gratitude for bearing with me as I persevered through my many years of triumphs and mistakes in managing money. Her support helped turn my business and my analytical process into what it is today. When I told her I was going to write another book — on top of all of the other commitments I have at this stage in life — she was fully onside with the idea. I couldn't have done it without her.

Keith Richards

Keith has been in the securities industry since 1990. An early adapter to the field of Technical Analysis, Keith began using the discipline in the mid 1990's, ultimately becoming one of the early Canadian Portfolio Managers to obtain the CMT designation. He is President, Chief Portfolio Manager and founder of ValueTrend Wealth Management, which is a discretionary investment service for high-net-worth clients. Mr. Richards' articles and interviews appear regularly in *Investors Digest, The Moneyletter, MoneySaver*, the *Globe and Mail*, and other media sources. His appearances on BNN Bloomberg Television have been a mainstay on the program since its "Rob TV" days back n the 1990's. Mr. Richards' books, *SmartBounce: 3 Action Steps to Portfolio Recovery* and *Sideways: Using the Power of Technical Analysis to Profit in Uncertain Times*, are available in bookstores.

Introduction

Well over a decade ago, I wrote my first book " *SmartBounce: 3 Action Steps to Portfolio Recovery.*" That book, which was published in mid 2009, was written during the height of the 2008 bear market. My book SmartBounce contained lessons that I had learned during the market crash of 2001. Seven years later, I was able to apply those lessons during the 2008 market crash to drastically reduce downside risk. I was inspired to write about the strategy that allowed me, and the client portfolios that I managed, to limit risk during that 2008 crash. I wanted to extend a hand, so to speak, to investors who were mortified by their own losses that year. Some investors watched their portfolios deteriorate by up to half of their value. *SmartBounce* offered readers a strategy to recover portfolio losses and to prevent similar portfolio losses in the future.

Lessons from 2001

The 2001 bear market, often called the "Dot Com" crash saw a 50% decline on the S&P 500 between March of 2000 to October of 2002. The S&P fell from a high of 1553 to a low of 768 over 19 months. My clients and I were hit hard in 2001. The seemingly endless bull market during my early career in the 1990s had made me, and most investors, pretty complacent. It was easy to make money in the markets during the 1990s. Any fool could do it. Proof of that statement: This fool sure did!

I was fortunate enough to have started my career in the securities industry in 1990. I was a stockbroker, joyfully riding the bull market of the 90s with blue chip stocks. In the late 1990s my clients profited by owning the leading dot-com plays like Nortel, Juniper Networks and Intel. During my first decade in the business, the Canadian market (represented by the TSX 300 composite index) more than tripled, starting near 3000 in 1990 and peaking over 11,000 by 2001. Meanwhile, the S&P 500 index rose from around 300 in 1990 to over 1500 by 2001. That was more than a quadruple! Times were good for investors and their Advisors. "Buy & hold" became the mantra. After all, markets only go up, right?

An easy market and big commissions — particularly coming from a growing investment class of "DSC" (Deferred Sales Charge) mutual funds — attracted many people seeking careers in the financial industry. At the bottom of the Investment Advisory heap were the Advisors with MFDA licenses (Mutual Fund Dealers Association of Canada). These folks typically called themselves "Financial Planners," despite holding no credentials beyond licenses to sell mutual funds. Later, the MFDA insisted any Advisor wishing to use the title Financial Planner acquire a CFP (Certified Financial Planner) designation. Certification or not, these Advisors were restricted to selling mutual funds, supplementing that income with high commission paying insurance products. Even fully licensed IROC (Investment Regulatory Organization of Canada) Advisors eventually jumped on the mutual fund bandwagon. These funds had high management expenses — typically 2.5% per year — and paid Advisors a lucrative built-in sales commission. Advisors sold them through a crafty contract that tied investors into the funds for up to seven years. This was done through a strategy known as the "Deferred Sales Charge." Investors who sold their funds before the seven-year holding period were penalized. The high management expenses would normally crush your returns. But in an environment of 10%-15% annual market returns, those 2.5% management expenses were easily hidden.

The bull market of the 1990s inspired unrealistic expectations by investors and their Advisors. Few investors considered the fact that long termed returns were actually closer to 8% on the markets. Investors were convinced that double-digit gains were the new norm for stock markets. Investment Advisors, through the benefit of a hot market, looked like heroes to their clients. It didn't matter how unsophisticated an Advisors investment knowledge was. All any Advisor needed to do was get you into the market. You bought, you held. Investors and Advisors alike — we all felt like investment rock stars.

And then 2001 happened.

If only we had listened to Fed Chairman Alan Greenspan. On December 5, 1996, Greenspan criticized investors during the stock market boom — particularly as the technology bubble drove markets higher & higher in the late 1990s. His famous remarks of "irrational exuberance" were my first real awareness of using contrarian investor sentiment as an investment tool. Greenspan was right. The market was getting irrationally exuberant. Ironically, this irrationality is a condition that can provide awesome opportunities for those who understand the discipline of contrarian investing. If I only knew then what I know now …

Licking my wounds after the 2001 market crash, I resolved to never again be a victim of a severe market meltdown. I established an investment strategy based on the lessons learned though my 2001 losses.

In my book *SmartBounce*, I outlined a few of the basic investment tenants to help investors recover their investment losses and dampen the potential for future losses in the future. Those tenants included:

1. Following an asset allocation strategy (defined as the balance between stocks, bonds, cash and hard assets).

2. Understanding and investing within investment cycles and trends.

3. Investing in the right place at the right time by using Technical Analysis.

ONCE BITTEN, TWICE SHY:
How I was prepared for the CRASH of 2008

Looking back at the 2001 market crash, I realize now that it was the best thing that ever happened to me in my career. Mind you, it sure didn't feel like that at the time! Having to answer to distressed clients who had experienced more than 30% losses in their investment accounts sure didn't elevate my mood that year.

Little did I realize that by creating and following a strategy when it came to asset allocation, incorporating technical analysis rules, and following sector rotation strategies — I was preparing for another career changing moment.

By early 2003, stock markets entered a new bull market. The US S&P 500 index rose from its 2001 crash bottom level near 800 to well over 1500 by late 2007. Nearly a double in less than four years! The TSX was even stronger, driven by the energy markets. It rose by two and half times — the TSX 300 index rose from 6,000 in early 2003 to nearly 15,000 by early 2008; that's about 25% per year, annualized. Talk about irrational exuberance! High double-digit returns were back on the table. This time it was the energy markets, REIT's, and mortgage-backed securities delivering the returns. Investors and their Advisors, quickly forgetting the lessons learned during the 2001 technology boom and bust, jumped right back on the bull market bandwagon. Returns of 10%–15%+ were the order of the day.

By 2007, I had attained my Portfolio Managers license. I was running a discretionary investment model for my clients that incorporated technical analysis and contrarian trading strategies. Although I was a Vice President within a big bank firm at the time, I still was allowed to use the trademarked name "ValueTrend" to differentiate my investment approach. That name stuck. In early 2008, I left the bank and established ValueTrend Wealth Management. Talk about timing — I left the security of my bank job just as the market began to implode! However, thanks to my 2001-inspired investment rules as outlined in *SmartBounce*, I was one of the few people who managed to substantially reduce that volatility. Sure, the ValueTrend Equity Platform declined as the market crashed, but nowhere near as much as the market did. In 2007, I raised cash and lowered my market beta by reducing exposure to the hot sectors of the time. Despite a market meltdown of more than 50% on most major North American indices, the ValueTrend Equity Platform experienced significantly less downside. Moreover, the portfolio recovered fully within a year of the March 2009 bottom. Meanwhile, the S&P 500 took until mid 2013 to recover its old highs. How did I pull that feat off? Well, some of the clues of the overbought market were mirroring those leading into the 2001 crash. I had learned my lesson in 2001 and had incorporated a few sentiment indicators and stop-loss rules in order to reduce my chances of being hit hard again.

In fact, my success during the 2008 crash inspired me to write a second book to cover the subject of Technical Analysis more thoroughly. I wanted to discuss the indicators, chart analysis techniques and trading rules not covered in my first book, *SmartBounce*. In 2010, I wrote a book allowing ordinary investors to understand the discipline of Technical Analysis. I discussed how to use the tools of Technical Analysis to reduce the risk of your portfolio. It covered how I reduced the risk of the portfolios I managed during the 2008-2009 market crash. In 2011, *Sideways: Using the Power of Technical Analysis to Profit in Uncertain Times* was published. Retail investors appreciated the straightforward pragmatic guide to Technical Analysis of the book. I'm still humbled by the positive feedback on Amazon for *Sideways*.

In *Sideways*, I covered the most important tools for investors to consider when discovering new investment candidates. More than just buying securities at the right time, it offers strategies on when to sell them. The book covered trend and phase identification, momentum oscillators, moving averages, cycles, and Japanese candlestick formations. It briefly touched on contrarian investing, as did my first book *SmartBounce*. But it really wasn't enough of a comprehensive look at contrarian investment tools. In fact, I've not been able to find many pragmatic books strictly focusing on this important aspect of investing. While there are books out there on contrarian investing, I have yet to find one covering the new tools available for contrarian investors and how to incorporate these tools into a well structured investment strategy. This book addresses that need.

The markets have changed since my first two books. Things happen so much faster these days. Markets rise hard, and fall harder than they every have before. Timely stock market news flow and access to relatively sophisticated analysis tools were once exclusive to investment professionals. These tools are now easily available to retail investors through the Internet — often at no cost. That's a big change from when I was a retail broker during the 1990s.

And yet, some things remain the same. Human nature sure hasn't changed. We humans are still hardwired with an instinct to follow the crowd, as I outlined in *Sideways*. Despite the access to on-demand financial news and a plethora of analytical tools and trading platforms — we are still driven by an age-old desire to follow the herd. Knowing that the instinct to follow the crowd in almost all aspects of life will remain within the human species for the foreseeable future is key in understanding why contrarian-investing strategies provide an edge — now, and in the future. Sophisticated investors will continue to resort to their lizard-brains in moments of flight or fight, fear and greed, and other moments of high stress or emotion.

Normally, herd behaviour isn't such a bad thing in life. For example: When people are running away from a burning building, you might be well served to follow that crowd towards safety. Challenging herd behaviour by being contrarian and running into the building is usually the wrong decision. As sensible as that instinct is to join the crowd and run from that burning building, it's not always such a great instinct to follow the crowd when investing. Investors who follow the crowd trade often buy at market tops and sell at market bottoms. Following the herd at times like that is not going to help with your investment profitability. But how do we know when the crowd is wrong? My aim in this book is to help you step outside of the natural tendency to follow the crowd at the wrong time in the investment cycle. You want to follow the crowd when the trend is healthy, but you don't want to stay in the trade when it's become over-crowded and ready to roll over.

THE INVESTMENT CYCLE

The diagram below is one that you may have seen before. It represents the investment cycle, as driven by investor crowd behaviour. The cycle moves between bull markets and bear markets as investors rotate between the various stages of euphoria and despair.

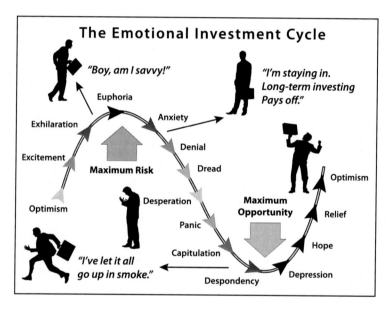

Figure 1: The Investment Cycle

While examining the investor behaviour cycle chart above, you may wonder how an investor can quantifiably identify euphoric market conditions that lead into market peaks. Conversely, you many wonder how we might identify declining markets near the capitation stage of a market bottom. Is there a way to identify which part of the behavioural cycle the market is currently in, and profit by these peaks of emotional buying and selling behaviours?

Jason Geopfert of SentimenTrader.com (you will be introduced to his work later in this book) suggests that market tops and market bottoms are often identified by a number of recurring traits. I'd recommend you keep the following lists handy as a "check list" to regularly ascertain market conditions. The more of the following conditions present, the more likely we are at or near a market top:

- **High optimism**
- **Easy credit (*too* easy, with loose terms)**
- **A rush of initial and secondary offerings**
- **Risky stocks outperforming quality stocks**
- **Stretched valuations**

Goepfert suggests that market bottoms also coincide with reoccurring traits. As with market topping conditions, the more conditions for the list below that present themselves, the more likely we are at or near a market bottom:

- **Extreme pessimism**
- **Oversold breadth (few stocks moving up vs. moving down)**
- **Risky stocks crash**
- **Negative media coverage**
- **Credit slams shut**

INSTINCT vs. ANALYSIS

Some investors like to think they have good "instincts," allowing them to discern when markets are irrationally pessimistic or exuberant. Perhaps they actually do have some level of "market mojo," steering them in the right direction when things have gone too far in one direction or another. I'm not one of those gifted people. I need hard and fast rules, quantitative evidence, and informed decision making tools to guide me. If you aren't one of those gifted clairvoyants either, I'm sure that this book will increase your investment success by quantitatively identifying opportunistic moments within the investment cycle. You'll discover unique tools that can help you identify opportunities to aid you in buying when broad markets, sectors and even individual stocks have entered into their fear-phase. You'll learn to use tools that will help you sell into markets that have entered into their euphoria phase.

Sure, some of the factors in the two models noted above can be observed through your day-to-day observations as an investor. Credit availability and bullish or bearish media coverage, for example, are observable by most investors. But we'll need more than just casual observations to make accurate buy/sell decisions on today's fast moving markets. With that in mind, we'll be talking about quantitative methods to measure some of the other factors noted above. By the time you finish reading this book, you will have some reliable strategies to aid you in beating the crowd through contrarian investing.

CHAPTER 1

When Contrarian Investing Works, and When It Doesn't

In the Monty Python comedy movie *Life of Brian*, an ever-growing crowd of worshipers is harassing the central character, Brian. Brian is thought by the crowd to be the next messiah, despite his refusal to acknowledge the title. Having reached the point of maximum frustration with his unwanted celebrity, he urges the crowd to stop following him. In a speech to his followers, he asks them to seek refuge not in himself, but in their own individualism. Here is a transcript of that scene from the movie:

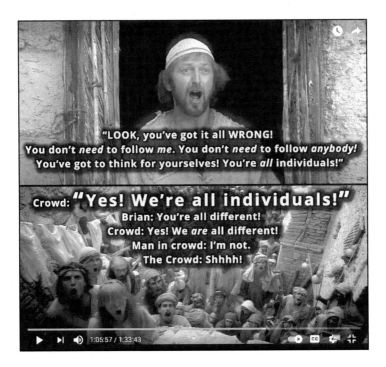

Figure 2: Scene from *Life of Brian* by Monty Python

We humans like to think that we are all unique individuals, like snowflakes. No two are alike. True, to a point. We're all somewhat unique. But not as much as you might think! After its inception in 1990, The Human Genome Project found a 99.9% similar genetic content between all humans. That study suggested that you and I are about 0.1% unique. Since the Human Genome Project, further research on the human genome has been conducted. Britain's Wellcome Trust Sanger Institute has uncovered a greater differentiator in human DNA. It estimates somewhere near 12% variation between the genes of different individuals. Whether we are 99% or 88% the same as each other — it is a fact that we have more in common than not.

Let's return to our snowflake analogy. Despite any uniqueness found in the shape of individual flakes, they have unfailing characteristics that make each flake part of the substance we call snow. Snowflakes tend to be white, cold, sticky, and melt when it gets warm. This, despite every flake's unique shape and size. Humans, too, vary in size, shape, skin tone, intelligence, etc. However, there are basic characteristics that define us as humans, making us more similar to each other than unique.

Because this book focuses on the psychology of investing, we'll spend time understanding one specific defining characteristic of human psychology. That characteristic is our tendency to "herd" — or follow the crowd. Christopher Hitchens notes in his book *Letters to a Young Contrarian*, "People have a need for reassurance and belonging." This basic instinct is derived from the limbic system in our brains. I covered this subject in my book *SmartBounce*, and I have reprinted that part of the book, where I reference the work of famed Technical Analyst Robert Prechter, below. It's a characteristic that defines us all.

Robert Prechter Jr. gives us a biological and psychological perspective in his book *The Wave Principal of Human Social Behavior* and the *New Science of Socionomics*. He provides insight as to why these patterns occur throughout human activity. He draws from the lifetime work of Paul MacLean, former head of the Laboratory for Brain Evolution at the National Institute of Mental Health. According to MacLean's work, the human brain can be divided into three main parts. These are: the *basil ganglia* which control impulses basic to survival, the *limbic system* which controls emotions, and the *neocortex* which is the seat of reason.

According to Prechter's book, the *limbic system* is hardwired for certain emotional and physical patterns of reaction to insure survival of the species. Impulsive *herding behavior* is derived from this portion of the brain and is similarly hardwired. Essentially, when facing an investment decision, independent thought is counter-intuitive. For example, even the most rigorous analysis systems are by no means going to give us certainty in judging where a security or market is headed. Thus, our subconscious tends to say to us: *you have too little basis upon which to exercise reason, thus the best alternative is to assume the herd is correct in its judgment!* Prechter then shows numerous studies of so-called "Smart Money" herding right along with the public in buying high/selling low. For example, mutual fund managers hold more cash at market bottoms (which is when they should be fully invested). Analyst's earnings forecasts exhibit positive or negative biases with disappointing accuracy near tops and bottoms.

Pressure from peers, whether perceived or real, may be one reason why people have difficulty taking an opposite investment stance to the crowd. Herding and mimicking can be self-preservative behaviors rooted in the limbic system of our brains. Prechter notes that a flock of poultry will peck to death any individual bird that has wounds or blemishes. In other words — it can be an instinctive advantage to survival to avoid rejection by signifying *I am like you.* This instinct can be difficult to fight when it comes to the somewhat stressful activity of investing on the markets.

Another example of the limbic system's importance is the instinct to run with the crowd when facing danger. Recall my example of a crowd running out of a burning building. Similarly, a herd of gazelles will uniformly run away from a lion on the African plains. Clearly, these crowd following behaviours illustrate the benefits of our built-in instinct to follow the herd.

Tattoos and Trucks

Beyond self preservation, our instinct to herd affects our decision-making on less important matters. Many of our actions are unknowingly driven by our instinct to follow others and to "fit in." As Prechter notes, we have a strong instinct to fit in with the crowd that is based on preservation instinct. By illustrating behaviour that differs too much from the crowd, we face potential criticism or even being ostracized by our peers.

For example, I was born in small-town Ontario in the early 1960s. The local church had a dominant presence in the town back then, although my parents were not religious. As such, my parents hadn't intended on christening me as a baby. Peer pressure to christen me was applied by my mother's peers & neighbours, including a visit at her door by the church minister. My mother feared criticism and ostracization if she didn't bend to peer pressure. Ultimately, she complied and proceeded with my baptism. My mother's decision to baptize me was based entirely on her need to "fit in" with the community.

We've all witnessed similar situations where we've felt the pressure of fitting into our own tribes. Try wearing a 1980s style wide tie in your office and enjoy the reactions of your peers. Try explaining your vegetarian diet to neighbours in small town Texas. Try being a staunch conservative if you live on the west coast of North America, or a staunch left-wing atheist in the "deep south." As Canadian rock group Rush sang in their song Subdivisions, " *Be cool or be cast out.*" The song relayed the experiences of band members Geddy Lee and Alex Lifeson who felt alienated during their teenage high school years.

The fashion industry has profited by our tribal desire to fit in for years. North Americans have long illustrated their desire to herd. This is seen in our automotive purchasing trends. Witness the move from family sedans, wagons and minivans of the 1980s and 1990s into less fuel-efficient and often less practical SUV's and Pickup trucks in the 2000s. Ford Motor Company announced they would discontinue producing sedans in 2020, focusing instead on trucks and SUV's. This will be the first time in the company's 120-year history (the company was founded in 1903) for the company to stop producing traditional family sedans.

Why these moves by Ford to sell trucks only? Lets follow a typical buying decision of a Ford truck customer. Your accountant or local real estate agent wants to drive the vehicle that his friends do. His friends drive pickup trucks. The billboard on the way to work paints a picture of a macho pickup truck driver traversing over boulders in the rough plains of Colorado. He likes this image. Deep inside he would like to be a little bit more like the guy in the billboard. The reality, of course, is that our accountant friend will never drive his vehicle over boulders in Colorado. He won't be loading it up with a payload of dent and scratch inducing building materials either. Instead, he'll drive his shiny new vehicle on paved highways. He'll keep this fashionably painted truck (volcanic orange with a stripe on the hood) pristine. Perhaps he'll keep with the in-crowd by adding width-enhancing wheel spacers, and possibly he'll even jack the suspension up. He's completed the rugged and macho image. Just like his buddies!

Your accountant is not making a unique or practical choice to buy a truck — despite his efforts to justify the purchase ("I haul the boat to the cottage once a year, so I need a truck all year round!"). His limbic system has driven him (pardon the pun) to fit in with the neighbours, and the current auto trends. He doesn't know that it's his herding instinct pushing him towards that decision. He thinks he's made the decision on his own. Just like in the Monty Python skit, he's part of the crowd shouting, "We are all individuals." He's not as much of an individual as he might think — at least in this decision.

A similar trend has occurred with the recent rise of tattoos. Up until the late 1990s, nary a person I knew had a tattoo. Except for bike gang members, prisoners, and a few groups such as military or tradesmen, most people had no interest in inking their skin. Suddenly, tattoos became all the rage. Rock stars and celebrities popularized the tattoo. The generations most influenced by these celebrities began to tattoo their own bodies. What began as a sign of differentiation by the early adapters, "inking" one's skin has turned into a sign of mass assimilation. While my generation (baby boomers) has not been quite as influenced by this herding behaviour — there's now barely a person under the age of 40 who *doesn't* have a tattoo.

Figure 3: Tattoo bearing millennial

Tattoo bearing millennials and baby boomer truck buyers share a commonality in their behaviours: They are following instinct-driven herding behaviour. Ironically, to be unique in these behavioural patterns, these fine folk must **not** ink their bodies, and (assuming they do not work in construction), they need to drive a sedan or mini-van rather than an SUV or truck. Be warned though: Should you fight those trends, you'll be fighting your own limbic system to follow the herd!

Why Contrarian Investing Works

In his book *Sapiens: A Brief History of Humankind*, Yuval Harai notes the primary drivers behind the dominance and survival of homo sapiens (that's us) and differentiates them from those of other humanoids. Some 100,000 years ago there were at least six other human species inhabiting the earth. One of the drivers behind the dominance of homo sapiens was the ability to communicate more effectively with one another. Beyond learning to effectively communicate within our own species, humans bonded with other species through communication. Dogs and cats developed unique relationships with humans because of their ability to communicate with us in a meaningful way. Meanwhile, creatures of even higher intelligence, such as pigs, remained nothing more than a food source due their inability to communicate effectively with human beings.

Harai notes that homo sapiens advanced as a species due to their ability to communicate through *storytelling*. As an example, rather than a few words with a jester indicating "danger over there," homo sapiens relayed a more memorable lesson through telling a tale. Perhaps that story went something like this: "I was out last night with Oalf and Org. Suddenly a pride of lions came upon us by the river. Oalf was eaten — but Org and I escaped!"

The story would be relayed through a combination of key words and jesters. This tale provided instructions to aid others in avoiding the specific danger of lions by the river at night. The continued development of language, stories and tales morphed into teachings, religion and persuasiveness. The power of story telling lives to this day through salesmanship, political persuasion, education and — you guessed it — investing.

Robert Shiller notes the effect of story telling on investors in his book *Narrative Economics: How stories go viral and drive major economic events*. His thesis suggests that ideas can go viral amongst investors through storytelling. Modern day story telling might include the new "green deal," and stock behaviour surrounding energy sources and electric vehicle makers. As the story grows amongst investors (whether the story be legitimate or overblown), its influence on the market grows. The crowd perceives a new paradigm that has permanently altered the market in one way or another.

American science writer Michael Shermer's book *The Believing Brain: From Ghosts to Gods to Politics and Conspiracies — How We Construct Beliefs and Reinforce Them as Truths* explains the neuroscience behind our beliefs:

> "The brain is a belief engine. From sensory data flowing in through the senses, the brain naturally begins to look for and find patterns, and then infuses those patterns with meaning. These meaningful patterns become beliefs. Once beliefs are formed, the brain begins to look for and find confirmatory evidence in support of those beliefs, which adds an emotional boost of further confidence in the beliefs and thereby accelerates the process of reinforcing them — and round and round the process goes in a positive feedback loop of belief confirmation."

Big picture stories are spread through a combination of influences. Tales of investment success are spread between individuals through word of mouth. Meanwhile, the media verifies and amplifies the stories. The story grows, aided by social media posts, discussion groups, and tweets. A few examples of crowd-made mega booms include:

- **The Internet & technology expansion excitement of the late 1990s (bandwidth expansion will drive internet provider stocks sky high!)**
- **Peak Oil Theory in the early 2000s (oil to $200/barrel!)**
- **The 2018-2020 FAANG overvaluation (Facebook, Apple, Amazon, Netflix, Google)**
- **"Stay inside" stocks after the COVID-19 pandemic broke out**
- **Clean energy and EV stocks like Tesla hype in 2020**
- **Crypto currencies boom and bust in 2017**
- **The cannabis boom and bust in 2019**

I'm not implying that any or all of the above market moves are, or were, doomed to fail. In fact, many investment themes, such as the move towards a technology driven economy, turned out to be true. Many hyped up market themes will result in prosperity over time. But many will not.

Legitimate or not, when such an idea attracts a flurried interest by the masses, herd behaviour takes over. Even a legitimate investment theme or story can drive stock prices to overbought (or oversold) levels. Even if it's just temporary.

Robert Shiller is not the originator of investment trends linked to story-telling. Gustave Le Bon, in his book written in 1895 called *The Crowd: A study of the popular mind*, noted that the primary characteristic of a crowd is its "susceptibility to contagious suggestion." The now departed intel-lectual, Christopher Hitchens, echoed this thought in his book Letters to a young contrarian: "People in the mass or the aggregate often have lower intelligence than their constituent parts." In other words, just because the crowd is in on a trade, doesn't mean you should join in …

Here's why:

Good idea or not, an overcrowded trade leaves little upside until ratio-nality returns to the market. Picture an overcrowded trade to be a little like an overcrowded elevator. An elevator will only hold so many people. Cramming more people into that little space will put the entire group in danger of catastrophic failure. The problem with a story-driven invest-ment theme is that, unlike an elevator, there's no sign on the door for investors to know what the maximum upside capacity of a stock trade is going to be.

Perhaps you have heard of the Greater Fool Theory (GFT). This philosophy states that it's okay to be a bit foolhardy when buying into a crowded investment theme. A proponent of the GFT acknowledges they are a fool to buy into a crowed trade. But they are betting that a Greater Fool than they are will eventually buy the security at a higher price. It is only when the Greatest Fool(s) has/have bought that the price of the secu-rity peaks. You could reverse that philosophy by saying that the price of a security bottoms when the Greatest Fool has capitulated and sold.

As contrarian investors, we don't want to be the last investor into the overcrowded elevator. We don't want to be the Greatest Fool when buying or selling a stock. The tools in this book will offer insight into how the greater fools are investing. We'll examine tools to help you avoid being part of that foolish crowd when you invest. Moreover, we'll discuss strate-gies to *profit* from their foolishness! We'll look at ways to identify when the time is right to be buying underpriced stocks when the crowd has foolishly sold. We'll examine ways to determine when its time to sell — or avoid overpriced stocks when the crowd is foolishly buying.

Contrarian Investing and Investment Decisions

Contrarian investment tools are useful beyond the longer lasting investment themes like Peak Oil Theory or the Dot-Com bubble. For example, the –35% COVID market crash in March of 2020 took no more than three weeks to complete its peak to trough decline for the S&P 500. The world looked to be coming to an end that March and (so the crowd thought), the economy and stock markets would be suppressed for years to come. The investment crowd threw in the towel on stocks, and hoarded toilet paper and paper towel instead.

Then things changed. The 35% stock market crash with a doom and gloom forecast for the economy in March reversed. One month later, by April 30, investor sentiment had evolved into an optimistic view on a new "stay at home" economy. Five months after the crowd had cut markets aggressively, stocks like Zoom, Peleton, the FAANGs and other stay-at-home stocks had doubled, or more. Investments benefitting from the stay-at home pandemic policies skyrocketed. Their capitalization within major stock market indices like the S&P 500 increased dramatically. By August 2020, a new high on the S&P 500 had been reached. "Rejoice!" said investors. Everyone will work at home and prosperity will grow thanks to the efficiencies of stay-at-home technology. Talk about a reversal in extremes of investor sentiment!

Interestingly, many of the tools we'll talk about in the next chapter presented significant buy signals at the March 2020 bottom of the COVID crash. You'll learn about contrarian buy and sell signals provided by some very reliable tools available to any investor.

When Contrarian Investing Doesn't Work

There are tools available for contrarian investors looking for signals of overcrowded or under-owned trading opportunities. We will cover many of them in this book. However, like most good trading indicator, these tools do not work in all situations. For example, contrarian indicators will not foretell black swan events. Most observers define a black swan event as an event that is rare, very significant, and impossibly difficult to predict. Interestingly, most black swan events are considered obvious in hindsight.

Black Swan events are market-influencing occurrences. The North American COVID virus outbreak in early 2020 was a Black Swan event. Interestingly, COVID had already been spreading "virally" (pardon the pun) throughout its country of origin, China. Travellers leaving China brought the virus to countries throughout developed and emerging nations worldwide. As the Back Swan definition suggests, the COVID outbreak in North America, like many Black Swan events, now appears "obvious" in hindsight.

Unlike the COVID crash, many boom and bust market cycles were at least somewhat predictable. For example, there were reliable contrarian sell signals coming into the 2001 dot-com market crash. Contrarian sentiment indicators such as the Put/Call ratio hit extreme levels of complacency. That indicator provided ample warnings ahead of the technology crash. The extent of that crash was magnified by the Black Swan event during the September terrorist attacks in New York City and Washington. While the dangerous exuberance of the stock market bubble was identifiable by quantitative analytical tools, there was no way that most investors would be able to prepare for a terrorist attack. Again, as with all Black Swan events, hindsight shows us that terrorist activity was on the rise throughout most of the developed world. It was only a matter of time before it would come to North America. That's hindsight for you! Unfortunately, I know of no tools that can monitor the entirety of world-wide activity in search of potential Black Swan events. We can, however, quantitatively monitor typical crowd behaviour to identify opportunistic, or dangerous trading environments.

One such example was the stock market crash of 2008. During that market meltdown, we witnessed the near collapse of the American banking system. We witnessed the almost unfathomable destruction of Lehman Brothers. The market crash of 2008-2009 brought with it a housing collapse, a near banking collapse, massive consumer credit defaults, and the destruction of a new class of loans known as "sub-prime mortgages." Out of desperation, major financial institutions — previously the lords of their own dominions, merged together for survival. It was like watching a row of dominos fall one at a time — with no idea just how far that row would continue collapsing before the destruction ended.

Were there any warning signs to the 2008 crash? Actually, yes, there were. As with the 2001 tech bubble implosion, contrarian sentiment indicators signalled an overbought market coming into 2008. I noted in the forward to this book that I came out of the 2008 crash ahead of the crowd thanks to the lessons I learned by losing money in 2001! My use of sentiment indicators and the actions taken resulting from their signals reduced my downside during the 2008 crash considerably. For example, the VIX indicator was deep into its "complacency zone" from 2005-2007, and it had alerted me to that risk, if not the precise timing of the top. Parabolic chart angles and breadth concentration heightened my awareness of danger. We'll discuss this and other indicators in the next chapter.

Despite the use of contrarian indicators, I still experienced some losses on the markets during the 2008 market crash. I certainly didn't foresee the *extent* of that bear market. Had my crystal ball been able to accurately and assuredly predict the timing and the extent of the crash, I would have exited the markets completely. It should be noted that if you think that there is a sure-fire way to accurately predict the timing and extent of a market crash, you are in for a rude awakening. Contrarian indicators and trend following rules simply increase your odds of trading success.

These techniques don't come with a guaranteed outcome. Were they able to offer such a guaranteed level of success, I would have gone 100% cash in early 2008, then re-bought in March of 2009 at the bottom. But of course, I didn't do that. We all know that there is no sure thing in trading. We can increase our odds of success by making a decision to reduce, not eliminate, equity exposure or equity beta (which is the comparative performance of a security to the overall market) when contrarian indictors signal market complacency. That's what I was doing in the first quarter of 2008. But there's no sure thing, and complacency signals will not work 100% of the time. By holding some exposure to stocks, you will not miss the entire upside move if markets move up despite a contrarian indicator risk signal. This book is not about becoming clairvoyant enough to perfectly time everything — it's about increasing your odds of achieving success.

Risky contrarian indicator signals coinciding with basic Technical Analysis selling rules allow us to raise cash and reduce exposure to overbought sectors. We can then wait for a re-entry signal from our trend and sentiment tools to redeploy our cash.

The market showed clear signs of irrational exuberance and speculation leading up to 2008. That gave me the heads-up to the danger. I got those re-entry signals in the spring and summer of 2009. The ValueTrend Equity Platform was entirely whole by early 2010 — three years before the S&P 500 reached that status.

Of course, the extent of any pullback will always be unknown. Traditional Technical Analysis sell rules as discussed in the final chapter of this book, and in my book *Sideways,* will provide you with the tools for the timing of exiting and entering the markets in an overcrowded environment. They have helped me sell into declining markets like 2008, and other smaller declines. They've helped me buy back into markets when the risk is lower.

This book will concentrate on combining contrarian investment tools with traditional Technical Analysis. I'll cover some of the basics in the Technical Analysis discipline through this book, but I'd encourage you to read my book *Sideways* for a better understanding of that discipline.

CHAPTER 2

Traditional Sentiment Indicators

"To buy when others are despondently selling and to sell when others are avidly buying requires the greatest fortitude."

— **John Templeton**

Anyone who follows sentiment studies will know that crowd sentiment is considered a contrarian indicator. When "everyone" loves a market or security — it's probably near the time to sell. Conversely, if "everyone" hates it, it might be near time to buy. Baron Rothschild once said that the time to buy is "when the blood is running in the street." That's a gruesome play on this contrarian way of looking at things.

Contrarian investors attempt to discover the inflection point that leads into a reversal in market direction — particularly when markets are priced at the extreme end of an overvalued or undervalued status. Contrarian investing relies on the myopic viewpoint of herding investors who project a market extreme as a new, permanent reality. As most people who have lived long enough realize, when an opinion of any type reaches an extreme, it tends to correct itself over time. Nothing lasts forever. Eastern philosophies like Buddhism and Taoism have known about this law of impermanence for centuries.

Contrarian Buy-Signals

A contrarian investor attempts to profit by *buying* into an oversold (or under-loved) stock, sector or market. Crowd pessimism is the contrarian buyer's friend. Stories abound regarding the terrible new reality facing the economy or market sector. That's how you make money during a market bottom. Market participants believe that things have changed for the worse on a permanent basis. Inventors who originally held a long termed investment strategy are systematically throwing in the towel. Contrarian investors look for signs of "capitulation" by the crowd. Some sort of crescendo in selling typically identifies capitulation bottoms. In this chapter, we will be examining tools that can help identify these inflective moments of opportunity. The interesting thing about contrarian indicators is that they are based off of human psychology. Things change, but peoples emotional reactions to situations remain predictable. That's why Sir John Templeton advised us to trust in the never-ending cycle of investor emotions illustrated in chapter one: "The investor who says, 'This time is different' has uttered among the four most costly words in the annals of investing."

Contrarian Sell-Signals

Contrarian investors don't just buy into oversold markets. They are also on the lookout to **sell** into an overbought, over-loved market. Irrational exuberance within the crowd is the contrarian seller's friend. At market tops, stories abound as to the future potential of the stock, sector or market. It is clear to these market participants that things have changed permanently. A new product, service or economic reality negates traditional valuations, earnings multiples or price behaviours. "This time is different" becomes the mantra of the crowd as they enthusiastically buy into the market, sector or stock. As with market bottoms, some sort of crescendo in buying occurs near market tops. We will examine tools in this book to help us identify these inflective moments of risk.

How Far is "TOO" Far?

We want to *buy* into capitulation/oversold markets. We want to *sell* into overcrowded/overbought trades. We are looking for market movements that have been driven by the irrationality of the crowd. To do this, we can't just assume that the crowd is wrong. After all, markets go up or down due to trending herd behaviour. Instead of investing against a trending market, we need a systematic, or quantitative approach to help us quantify those moments when herding investors are "too extreme" in their opinion. After all, the crowd can drive a market higher and higher (or lower and lower) for extended periods of time. The supposed "new paradigm" they are excited about can circulate and accelerate for months, or even years.

Take a look at any major market crash. The story starts with a belief in a new-paradigm. For example, in the late 1990s the story was that of growing need for technology Internet bandwidth. The crowd was correct in its belief in the growing need for technology. But its enthusiastic behaviour drove prices and valuations on technology stocks higher and higher over many years. This ultimately created a stock market bubble, and a crash. But the crowd pushed things up for quite some time before the inevitable market implosion occurred.

Similarly, the story of ever-expanding housing market and easy credit created the financial crisis and market crash of 2008. The story behind any bubble or bust can circulate and grow for extended periods of time before reversing. We certainly don't want to "fade the trade" (move opposite to the trade) before momentum has reached its crescendo. In fact, it's best to enter a trade when it appears that the current trend is starting to reverse.

In other words, just because a contrarian indicator flashes a level of investor complacency that has historically leaded into a correction, this does not imply that you should immediately sell the market. A contrarian indicator typically gives a heads-up to an oversold or overbought situation. They are often "leading indicators," rather than "coincident indicators." Some indictors, like the VIX (covered later in this chapter), can often provide this heads-up warning on a fairly timely basis. But the majority of these studies, like the investor confidence surveys (also discussed later in this chapter), signal a month — or more — ahead of a reversal.

A contrarian indicator signalling high levels of investor complacency indicates that conditions are ripe for a pullback, or a period of consolidation. These indicators signal potential changes in market behaviour before an actual reversal in trend in the underlying markets price. Conversely, a contrarian indicator signalling evidence of capitulation and fear during a selloff suggests that conditions are ripe for a turnaround. In both of these cases, there may be no evidence of a price reversal at the time of the signal.

Many sentiment indicators are leading indicators. This means that the market may continue to trend in an environment of exuberance (or fear) for days, weeks, or even months before an actual reversal occurs. It is for this reason that you should generally hold off on fading a stock or market when you get a contrarian signal. Instead, you will want to incorporate a technical trend signal to more accurately time your decisions. This famous quote by Maynard Keynes echo's my sentiment behind fighting price momentum and trends, despite clear signals of investor irrationality:

"The market can remain irrational longer than you can remain solvent."

— **Maynard Keynes**

Okay, lets say that you have received a heads-up for either a potential buying opportunity or a potentially selling indication from a contrarian indictor. Now, you should watch for changes in price behaviour by analyzing your other technical analysis tools. Perhaps you see a break in a key moving average in conjunction with an overbought or oversold momentum oscillator. In this way, you will exit or enter a market with the evidence of a contrarian signal *and* a price trend break — amongst other pieces of evidence. The final chapter in this book will examine a fictional investor who uses a logical Technical Trend Analysis approach, and contrarian investment strategy. You'll learn how combining the two disciplines will help you to make the best decisions in your entry and exit timing. This should help you to incorporate contrarian analysis tools within your own systematic approach to buying and selling.

TOOLS OF THE TRADE

In this chapter we will discuss 10 contrarian indictors to help you quantifiably identify moments of irrational exuberance or despondent capitulation by the crowd; in other words, we will be examining tools to help us identify when the majority of investors are "wrong." We'll examine how we can use these tools to become aware of overcrowded trades. As I did in my book *Sideways*, I have chosen to provide you with the indicators that I have personally found to be practical and accurate in this chapter. There are many more contrarian indicators available to investors than discussed in this book. Many of these indicators are available on the Internet via charting services. One of the best-known services out there is StockCharts. com. True, you can view their charts on the Internet at no cost, but the historic data and number of indicators are very limited with the no-cost tools available on the web. For less than $200 USD per year, you can subscribe to the basic StockCharts package and get access to all of their tools and many decades of historic data. I consider this type of charting service an essential investment that any serious investor should utilize.

I should also note that readers of this book who are serious about contrarian investing should consider getting at least a basic subscription to SentimenTrader. It's unbelievably cheap for the value it provides to contrarian investors. Yearly subscribers pay about $400 USD for access to most of their indicators. Even when subscribing to their basic service, SentimenTrader's site holds a plethora of contrarian indicators, along with notes on how to interpret them. Founder Jason Goepfert (whose interview with me will be highlighted in the next chapter) is the worlds leading provider of sentiment indicators. The website SentimenTrader.com offers indicators covering the broad US markets, individual countries, as well as sentiment indicators for stock sectors, bonds and commodities. Jason takes it a step further by providing a regular emailed research report highlighting his observations of market sentiment. That daily email is worth the price of the subscription on its own. I have no connection whatsoever to Jason's company beyond a subscription to his Premium service — which offers a few more contrarian indicators than the basic service. I believe that if you are truly serious about contrarian investing, you should at least buy a basic subscription to SentimenTrader. Consider it an investment in your trading success. For those who still don't want to subscribe to SentimenTrader, I have made an effort throughout this book to reference free sources of sentiment indicators on the web, where possible.

Throughout this book, I've chosen to cover many of the broad market contrarian indicators. While broad market sentiment indicators are more plentiful, I have covered some of the tools available for sector and individual security analysis. Thanks to services like SentimenTrader, you can examine crowd behavior surrounding international markets, US stock sectors, bonds, real estate, commodities and even individual stocks. Sentiment indicators are available for individual sectors as well as a huge variety of alternative assets and commodities.

Whether looking at macro-market sentiment indicators, or individual sector sentiment, what remains the same when viewing these contrarian investment tools is the reality of human nature. That is, the tendency for human beings to sometimes crowd into or out of markets, ultimately reaching the point of irrationality. Let's get started by looking at some of the most common contrarian investment tools available to investors.

TOOL #1: Price Chart Trend Angle

One of the challenges within traditional technical analysis lies in the spacing on a chart between the X (time) and Y (price) data plotted. If you adjust a weekly chart (for example) to depict 10 years of data on your computer screen, the angles of ascent and decent will differ from that of a three-year chart.

Trendlines also change within differing timeframes on a chart. Movements that appear significant on a three-year chart because of a trend line break will appear insignificant on a 10-year chart. The trendlines noted on your chart will take into account more data on a ten-year chart, making the moves over that longer term adhere to a different trendline.

Despite the inefficiencies of the time/price inefficiencies — you can still "eyeball" angles of ascent or decent over a *consistent* timeframe on any chart. For example, if you regularly track a market with 10 years of data on a weekly chart, you will easily be able to identify consistencies in the angle of accent or descent of normal market movements. In fact, by drawing trendlines, you'll be able to identify when the market has angled off of that trendline at an unusual velocity of ascent or decent. A dramatic price change that moves the market in question up or down in a short period of time will present itself as driven by emotional crowd behaviour. Watch for an extreme angle on the chart. If a market presents a drastically lower or higher price over a relatively short period of time that "arcs" off of a long-standing trendline, take note. Changes in market tempo often indicate a market that has been driven by fear or greed. The more extreme the movement, the more likely you are dealing with a fear/greed reaction by the crowd. An unusually strong movement on a chart can suggest an unsustainable reaction resulting from irrational exuberance or fear.

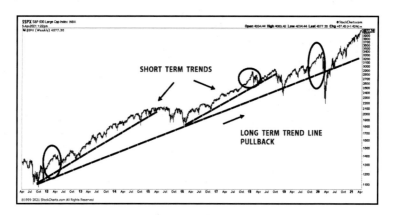

Figure 4: StockCharts — Parabolic chart angles on the S&P 500. Note how sharp angles of ascent (circled) tend to lead into pullbacks to the longer-term trendline.

KEITH G. RICHARDS

TOOL #2: Using Moving Averages to Spot Fear and Greed

Computing the average price of a security over a specific number of periods forms a simple moving average. Most moving averages use closing prices and drop the data from its first date as the average. This allows the moving average to "move" forward in time. Traditionally, moving averages are used to determine trend. However, I also use moving averages to determine if a market is getting too frothy, or too fearful. TOOL #1 referred to the price trend angle as a way of eyeballing whether a market is acting irrationally. You can take this methodology a step further by quantifying whether the angle of ascent or decent is "too steep" by measuring the move against a moving average, as I described above.

For example, let's say you are observing a longer termed trend on a stock or a stock index. You are tracking the trend of the index with the 200-day simple moving average (SMA). Note that the 200-day SMA is shown on a weekly chart as the 40-week SMA. You want to stay invested in the stock so long as it maintains a price that is above its 200-day (40 week) SMA. You might observe that sometimes the price of that security moves aggressively higher, arching off of the moving average significantly. You might notice that the market usually pulls the stock right back in line (closer to) the moving average whenever that happens. You might say that a longer termed moving average such as the 200-day version represents the mean, or average return on that security during its trend. A mathematically orientated person might call the pullbacks along that path as "regression to the mean."

Each stock or sector will have its own range of moving around its 200-day SMA before correcting. Smaller or less followed markets such as small-capped stocks will typically move aggressively above or below their key moving averages. Same goes with more volatile securities in biotech or commodity influenced stocks. Meanwhile, larger, more widely followed stocks or those in less volatile industries will illustrate smaller deviations off of their key moving averages. You will want to use a charting tool that measures the percentage moves from one point to another on a chart. You can use that tool to measure the moves of a security from the moving average you follow to get an idea of what constitutes an overbought move. For example, let's say that ABC stock has a typical range of no more than 10% over its 200-day SMA. If the stock moves 15% over that average, you may be looking at an overbought market that will correct back near its moving average. If the stock moves 20% over the moving average, you may be looking at a contrarian sell signal. The crowd has become frothy and has moved the stock too quickly.

I have found that if the S&P 500 moves ahead of its 200-day SMA by more than 10% it is starting to reach an overbought status. It's likely to correct a bit from such a move. Fifteen percent or higher indicates an increasing probability of an irrationally exuberant crowd. That's a sell signal in my books. I tend to reduce (not necessarily eliminate) my exposure to stocks in the managed accounts I have run for ValueTrend upon such a move.

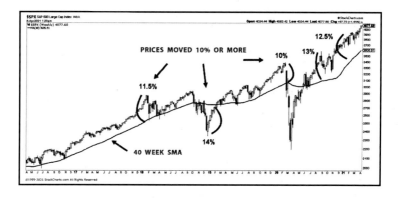

Figure 5: StockCharts — S&P 500 chart highlighting dates when prices moved 10% or more above or below the 40 week/200-day Simple Moving Average. Note how these moves typically signal an overbought or oversold market correction.

TOOL #3: The AAII

The AAII (American Association of Individual Investors) is a non-profit organization headquartered in Chicago, founded in 1978. Their stated mission is "assisting individuals in becoming effective managers of their own assets through programs of education, information, and research." It is affiliated with NAIC, the organization that helped so many investment clubs get started in the late 1990s.

The AAII surveys individual investors, and not professional traders or institutions. The survey is a weekly poll conducted by that organization which intends to gauge the overall sentiment of their membership. Membership is asked where they think the market will be in six months, and group the responses into three categories: bullish, bearish or neutral.

Like most contrarian indicators, when the survey shows too many investors as being bullish, it very often corresponds to market highs. Conversely, too many bears suggest that the market may soon find a low. Generally speaking, when the indicator goes too much above 2/3rds (66%) of their subscribers as bullish, it's a warning sign. Visa-versa for signals below 1/3rd of their surveyed subscribers as bullish — it's a bullish sign. Many online services post the indicator at no charge. SentimenTrader tracks the indicator as part of their package, and Investors Digest publication (whom I write for) prints the survey in each issue. It's available free on the AAII website at www.aaii.com/sentimentsurvey.

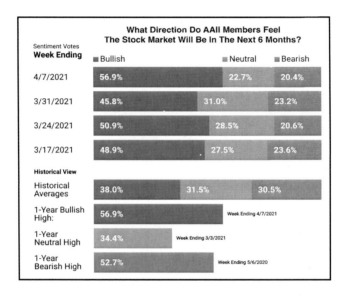

Figure 6: AAII Investor Sentiment Survey

TOOL #4: CNN Fear/Greed Indicator

The CNN Fear Greed index is a model created by and published by CNN on their public website. SentimenTrader has created a model based on the inputs discussed on the CNN website. The model measures inputs such as price trend, volatility, options trading, and bond trading to determine prevailing investor sentiment. It's interpreted in a similar way as other sentiment indicators and models, with rising optimism being good for stocks until it reaches extreme optimism, in which case it becomes a contrary indicator signalling an overbought market. The inverse is also true, with declining optimism being a negative for stocks until it reaches an extreme, in which case it begins being a contrary positive indicator. Beyond accessing the index through SentimenTrader's service, the index is available on the CNN website. CNN also offers a host of other free data points for the contrarian investor (https://money.cnn.com/data/fear-amnd-greed/).

Figure 7: CNN Fear & Greed Index chart

TOOL #5: AIM Advisor & Investor Survey

The Advisor & Investor Model (**AIM**) is a model unique to Sentimen-Trader's service. It consists of sentiment readings from several advisor and investor surveys. The index is computed on a weekly basis.

This model takes advantage of the fact that when the typical investor and investment advisor should be most bullish, they are most bearish. And, when the markets are getting overbought and are about to turn, these Johnny-come-lately are most bullish.

When a preponderance of the survey respondents are more bullish than they've been in the recent past, then the model will move towards its upper (red) trading band. When it approaches this band (or exceeds it), then we should be concerned that too many investors are expecting higher prices, have likely already bought, and therefore support for further prices gains is minimal.

When the model has moved towards or outside of its lower (green) trading band, then we know that investors have soured on the market's prospects to an extreme degree. This rarely lasts long, as the market has a strong tendency to rebound after such episodes. These signals are especially strong when the market tone is positive (e.g., the 40-week moving average of a broad index like the S&P 500 is rising).

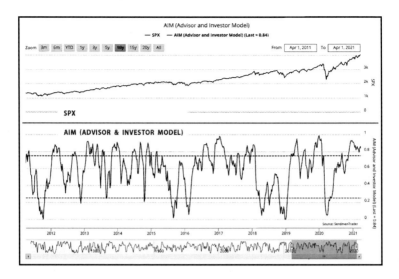

Figure 8: SentimenTrader.com — AIM Advisor & Investor Model chart vs. the S&P 500 can provide signals leading into market peaks and troughs, although the indicator's sensitivity leads into many false signals. For this reason, the AIM model is best used in conjunction with other indicators before reaching a conclusion on the sentiment status of the market.

TOOL #6: The CBOE Put-to-Call Ratio

The Put/Call indicator shows the ratio of call buyers versus put buyers on the CBOE (Chicago Board Options Exchange). As a refresher: investors who seek to profit or protect their position if the market on an underlying security falls buy puts. Investors who think the underlying security will rise buy calls. Greater demand for either puts or calls on a broad number of issues such as those in the S&P 500 reflects a change in overall bullishness or bearishness of that market. The Put/Call ratio is tracked by most online charting services. I use StockCharts.com.

A rising Put/Call indicator suggests an increasing volume in call options compared to put options. Conversely, a falling number indicates relatively decreasing call volume compared to puts. My research shows when the CBOE Put/Call indicator gets to around 0.75 (indicting 0.75 puts for every 1 call traded) for a few days in a row, the markets may be getting too bullish and are due for a correction. If the indicator moves above 1.25 (1.25 puts for every 1 call) for a few days, it suggests an oversold market that may be ready to rally.

Figure 9: StockCharts — CBOE Options total Put/Call ratio

TOOL #7: The CBOE Volatility Index

The VIX is another contrarian tool using options to read crowd behaviour. The CBOE Volatility index (VIX) predicts implied volatility of S&P 500 index options for the next 30 days. In essence, a high reading of the VIX indicator corresponds with higher market volatility and more costly options. A low reading of the VIX corresponds with lower market volatility and cheaper options.

The VIX is sometimes incorrectly referred to as the "fear index" (sometimes called the VIX the "vomit index" implying that high VIX levels indicate a sickly level of stress by market participants). Instead of being an indication of capitulation or overt bullishness, the VIX simply predicts volatility in either direction. High VIX levels suggest that options traders see significant potential for the market to move sharply, either up or down. Thus, you want to watch the VIX if you feel, based on your analysis; the market has become overextended in either direction. A market that appears to be over extended and making a top might be verified by a high VIX reading. Conversely, a market that has sold off aggressively and might be ready to bottom could also be backed by a high VIX reading. Truthfully, the VIX tends to make its extremes at the top end of its range when markets are declining. That's because, as the name "fear gauge" implies, investors panic with more enthusiasm than when they buy. As the old saying goes, "The market takes the stairs up, but it takes the elevator down." In other words, it panics faster than it rises. you rarely see a point where the VIX hits a high level while markets are rising.

I use StockCharts.com to track the VIX. High VIX levels — anywhere near 35 or higher — usually signal a market bottom or the end of a

KEITH G. RICHARDS

corrective period for stocks. That's because high VIX levels indicate capitulation and fear through overzealous volatility premiums by options traders. I've noticed that movements by the VIX above 25 very typically signal then end of short termed corrections.

Low VIX levels — somewhere near 12 or lower — signal a higher probability for a market correction, or the end of a bullish period for stocks. That's because a low VIX reading indicates a certain level of complacency by options traders. You can see these tendencies on the long termed VIX chart below.

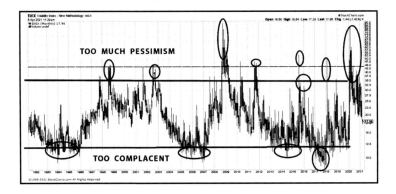

Figure 10: StockCharts — Volatility Index (VIX) Long-termed chart

TOOL #8: First Hour/Last Hour

In the 1990s, Merrill Lynch Canada's Technical Analyst Gurney Watson was tracking a technical analysis tool called the "Smart Money-Dumb Money" indicator (SMDM). He created his version of the indicator to track the movement of various US indices during two distinct time frames. These time frames are the first hours of trading (morning) and the last hours of trading (afternoon). Mr. Watson would chart the net gain or loss during the first two hours of the trading day, and compare it to the net gain or loss during the last two trading hours of the day. He labeled the trading done in the early part of the day as "Dumb Money" activity; the trading being done in the latter part of the day as "Smart Money" activity.

Dumb money is thought to move in the morning. Retail investors trade in reaction to recent news events or sentiment. They are reacting to very recent or even old news — myopically. Their knee-jerk trades can create sharp price movements in one direction. The first hour or so tends to be the most volatile period, providing plenty of sophisticated day traders to take advantage of this movement. Program trading reacts quickly to breaks in various moving averages on an intraday basis — adding to the fun.

Although it sounds harsh, professional traders often know that a lot of "Dumb Money" is flowing at this time. So do the program traders. The theory is that during the first part of the trading day, retail investors tend to execute trades based less on an analytical process, and more on an emotional, less sophisticated basis. Retail investors often base trades on recent news events and react quickly with fear or greed to their trading executions. These emotionally driven market movers are anxious to call their broker to execute their trades, within the first few hours of the day in response to the hot news of the moment.

Smart Money is thought to move the later part of the trading day. Stocks are ready to be scooped up by the pro's on the fear trade of earlier hours, or sold by the pro's based on knee-jerk bullishness. Theoretically, the selling pressure in the afternoon can be more significant as a predictive indicator than buying pressure in the afternoon. That's because of the longer termed bullish bias of stock markets to go up. Selling indicates a more unusual conviction by the Smart Money than does buying. Sophisticated traders, including market professionals, are more apt to trade using mechanical analysis programs to eliminate their emotions when making investment decisions. These investors are less inclined to react to their own fear and greed. According the SMDM theory, sophisticated traders take advantage of the rabid selling or buying done during the early hours of the trading day. By stepping in and buying (or selling) stocks from or to the early trading "dumb" sellers or buyers, they effectively "buy when others are despondently selling or sell when others are greedily buying," as Sir John Templeton once said. By the end of the day the net effect of the large buying or selling power coming from the professionals drives the market up or down in a direction opposite to the one created by the morning activity.

According to SMDM theory, the trick to determine which way the market might be heading in the near future is to watch the net movements of the indices during these periods of the day. Often, there is little consistency looking for patterns of SMDM movement when the market is either trending (up or down) or trading sideways. However, at market peaks and troughs, emotional trading in the morning escalates. The sophisticated investors begin to take advantage of this trading. Obviously, as investors, we are better to follow the "Smart Money" and fade, or do the opposite, of the "Dumb Money." When we look at morning vs. afternoon movements, the most important thing is to look for a pattern. If you see one day where the market goes down in the late afternoon after a relatively good start, that's probably nothing to get excited about. But a string of days where we get, say, four of the last five trading days with the market selling off in the last hour or two is a different story.

While tracking the First Hour/Last Hour isn't always a sure bet when looking for contrarian trading opportunities, you should still be aware of the concept. Suppose we notice over a period of trading days that there is a fairly obvious pattern of the smart afternoon money bidding the market higher than it was in the morning. This may be a sign that going long on the market is prudent. Conversely, if we see a pattern of afternoon markets moving lower than the morning, we might want to consider bearish strategies such as holding cash, hedging existing positions, or (for aggressive investors) shorting the market. You'll want to confirm your observations with other sentiment and technical indicators to see if there are other signs of an overbought or oversold market — but it can give you a heads up to a potential change in market direction.

Tracking this version of Smart Money versus Dumb Money can be done manually using an intra-day chart, comparing each day's first vs. last hour and looking for patterns. You can also track the first half of the day vs. the last half of the day, as illustrated in Figure 12. Or you can subscribe to www.sentimenttrader.com. They use the first half hour of the day's trading as "Dumb Money" and the last hour as "Smart Money."

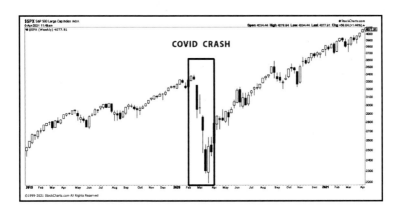

Figure 11: StockCharts — S&P 500 daily chart highlighting the March 2020 "COVID crash." The period between March 5th and March 23rd highlighted the peak-to-trough drawdown period.

Let's take a look at the March 2020 COVID crash to see if morning vs. afternoon trading movements gave us any clue as to when the markets were nearing their capitulation phase. Figure 11 illustrates the peak to trough drawdown on the S&P 500 between March 5th and March 23rd, 2020.

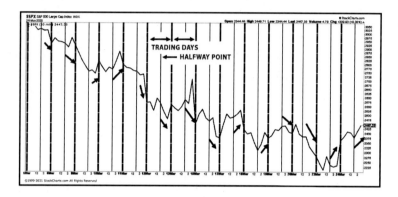

Figure 12(A): StockCharts — S&P 500 hourly chart highlighting the COVID crash between March 5th and March 23rd, 2020. Thick dashed vertical lines indicate the start of each trading day. The thinner lines represent the approximate halfway point for each trading day (12:30 pm). Note that traders were consistent sellers in the afternoons during the market meltdown (only on March 9th and 10th did they buy in the afternoon). Note the early positive confidence by traders on the afternoons on the 23rd and 24th. This signalled the bottom of the COVID crash.

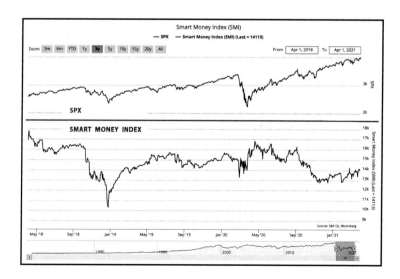

Figure 12(B): SentimenTrader — Smart Money Index (SMI). SentimenTrader does the work for you if you want to track the net returns of the first half hour vs. last half hour of the S&P 500 with the SMI. The way they calculate the index is to subtract the performance of the S&P 500 cash index during the first half hour of trading and to add the performance of the S&P during the last hour. I have found the first half hour vs. last half hour less valuable than the first half of the day vs. the last half as illustrated in Figure 12. For this reason, I tend not to use the SMI indicator.

Comparing the First Hour/Last Hour is one way to look at market movements, but you can also compare activity of the first half of the day to the last half of the day, as shown in Figure 12. On the chart you can see how traders were consistent sellers in the afternoons during most days of the COVID crash. This may have indicated that "Smart Money" was correctly selling with the anticipation of more downside to come. However, early positive confidence by traders in the afternoons on the last two days of the crash seems to have provided a heads up to a pending bottom.

TOOL #9: SentimenTrader's Smart Money/Dumb Money Indicator

The Smart Money Confidence and Dumb Money Confidence indices are a unique innovation by SentimenTrader. I must say that this indicator is my favourite amongst the various contrarian investment tools I use. It's a fascinating too that allows subscribers to see, in one quick glance, what the "good" market timers are doing with their money compared to what "bad" market timers are doing. I've taken the liberty to more or less copy the description of the indicator from their site, with a few of my own edits for clarity.

Examples of some Smart Money indicators that are included in the indicator are the OEX Put/Call and open interest ratios, commercial hedger positions in the equity index futures, and the current relationship between stocks and bonds.

Generally, we want to follow the Smart Money traders when they reach an extreme — we want to bet on a market rally when they are confident of rising prices, and we want to be short (or in cash) when they are expecting a market decline. The higher the confidence number, the more aggressively we should be looking for higher prices.

In contrast to the Smart Money, we want to do the opposite of what the

Dumb Money is doing when they are at an extreme. These traders have proven themselves over history to be bad at market timing. They get very bullish after a market rally, and bearish after a market fall. By the time the majority of them catch on to a trend, it's too late — the trend is about to reverse. It tells us how confident we should be in selling the market.

Examples of some Dumb Money indicators include the equity-only Put/Call ratio, the flow into and out of the Rydex series of index mutual funds, and small speculators in equity index futures contracts. SentimenTrader tracks both groups independently on one graph, where you can see to contrasts between their confidence levels. The company also charts the spread between Smart Money and Dumb Money. This gives us a quick view of the difference between the two groups of traders. Because the "Dumb Money" follows trends to their extreme, and the "Smart Money" generally goes against overdone trends, the "Dumb Money" is usually correct during the meat of the trend. So when the Dumb Money Confidence is higher than the Smart Money Confidence, that means sentiment is positive.

When it becomes "too" positive, however, then sentiment has reached an extreme, and stocks often run into trouble. This usually happens because the Dumb Money confidence rises above 60%, and the Smart Money drops below 40% confidence. That is a warning sign for stocks.

When the Dumb Money is below the Smart Money, then sentiment is negative and stocks are usually struggling. It's best to be defensive at times like this. However, when sentiment becomes too negative, then stocks are often poised to rally over the next one-to-three months.

What is considered "smart" is simply based on an indicator's historical record at extremes. If an indicator is usually showing excessive pessimism near a market peak, and excessive optimism near a market bottom, then that indicator will be included in our Smart Money calculation. And if it consistently shows too much pessimism near a low and too much optimism near a high, it will be considered Dumb Money.

Confidence indices are presented on a scale of 0%-to-100%. When the Smart Money Confidence is at 100%, it means that those most correct on market direction are 100% confident of a rising market, and we want to be right alongside them. When it is at 0%, this means that these good market timers are 0% confident in a rally, and we want to be in cash or even short when confidence is very low.

We can use the Dumb Money Confidence in a similar, but opposite, manner. For example, if the Dumb Money Confidence is at 100%, then that means that these bad market timers are supremely confident in a market rally. And history suggests that when these traders are confident, we should be very, very worried that the market is about to decline. When the Dumb Money Confidence is at 0%, then from a contrary perspective we should be concentrating on the long side, expecting these traders to be wrong again and the market to rally.

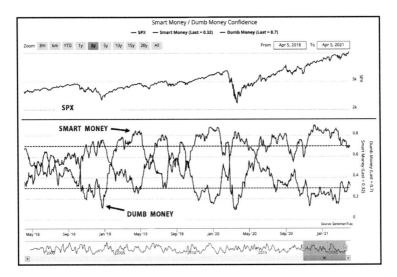

Figure 13: SentimenTrader — Smart Money/Dumb Money Confidence. Extreme levels of opposing confidence levels are signalled by the two groups crossing the respective high and low confidence level horizontal lines. Such extreme divergences between Smart & Dumb money can provide advance signals of market peaks and troughs.

I use the Smart Money/Dumb Money Confidence Spread, also by SentimenTrader, in my system. This indicator simply combines the ratio of confidence two groups and tracks their differentials as one single line. The bottom of the chart has a bearish horizontal line. This indicates that Dumb Money is 60% confident, and the Smart Money confidence has dropped below 40%. The lower the score on the chart, the greater the differential between Smart and Dumb Money confidence. You can reverse that mixture (40/60 confidence) for the upper, higher risk zone. The indicator reads as -0.25 for comparatively high confidence by Dumb Money, and 0.25 for comparatively high confidence of Smart Money. Below or above those levels are bearish/bullish signals.

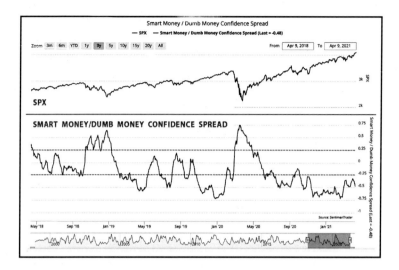

Figure 14: SentimenTrader — Smart Money/Dumb Money Confidence Spread. The spread between Smart & Dumb confidence levels provides an easy to interpret system to track the extremes seen on Figure 13. Note that market bottoms are accurately signalled by this spread much of the time. However, Dumb Money (retail investors) can remain irrationally exuberant for longer periods of time than they will remain despondent. As such, periods such as the post-COVID crash rally can push the two groups towards opposing views for many months at a time before a market correction.

TOOL #10:   Sector OPTIX Studies

SentimenTrader does a number of sentiment "OPTIX" readings on stock/bond indices, commodities and currencies. OPTIX indicators take sentiment data from six independent sources, and rank the studies is showing as to how pessimistic vs. optimistic various market players are. OPTIX studies are a compilation of "Smart Money/Dumb Money" studies by the following sources:

- **Market Vane Corporation**

- **Consensus, Inc.**

- **Daily Sentiment Index**

- **Larry Williams**

- **Bloomberg**

- **Ned Davis Research, Inc.**

An OPTIX is created using the data from the above sources to average out the overall sentiment readings. OPTIX charts go back a couple of decades or longer in most cases. That's enough data for us get a good handle if a market is in a good position for a turnaround. Like we saw in **TOOL #9**, bullish OPTIX readings are based on extreme levels of pessimism by the wrong groups of investors. An OPTIX can also signal if a market looks likely for a correction based on too much exuberance by those same groups.

OPTIX studies can include broad market indices, commodities, the bond markets, and currencies. They can be valuable tools when evaluating strategies regarding your current holdings (e.g. — whether to add to a position, hold, or look for a technical exit signal). SentimenTrader provides back-tested buy and sell zones for the sectors covered by their OPTIX readings. Generally, the sector is out of favour with the crowd when the OPTIX reading penetrates its lower horizontal line. This can be a bullish indicator. The crowd has overbought the sector if the indicator penetrates its upper horizontal line. That's a bearish signal.

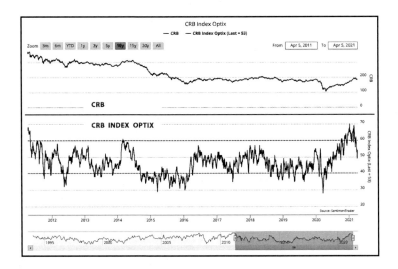

Figure 15: SentimenTrader — CRB (Commodity Research Bureau) OPTIX. Excessive optimism and pessimism signals provided plenty of advance notice of market peaks and troughs for this index.

OPTIX charts are a great way of spotting potential opportunities within under loved stock sectors and asset classes. By analyzing sectors with low or average sentiment readings, you can then look for positive technical trends or consolidation breakouts on their price charts. This use of technical analysis can get you in early on a breakout or uptrend before the crowd gets too enthusiastic.

Conversely, you should keep an eye on the OPTIX charts of the sectors and ETF's that you own in your portfolio for potential sell signals. I tend to monitor OPTIX sentiment on sectors I hold in my Managed Portfolios. Like I suggest you do with buying opportunities presented on OPTIX charts, I recommend you only make strategic sell decisions upon a technical trend breakdown coinciding with a bearish OPTIX score, rather than reacting to an unfavourable OPTIX sentiment reading alone.

Moving with the Times:
An interview with JASON GOEPFERT of SentimenTrader

The popularity with individual investors using research and tools available on the Internet lead into a new wave of investor enlightenment. Still, a little knowledge can be a dangerous thing. Ever growing access to information, along with increased availability of a plethora of investment opinions has created periods of heightened volatility on the markets. The increasing popularity in momentum trading via cheap online trading platforms has invited an entirely new type of retail investors into the fray. Institutional investors, who focus on fundamental valuation metrics and growth prospects, are being challenged in their domination of market insight.

One leading drive towards the rise of the retail investor's influence on stock market behaviour has been the popularity of app-based brokerages such as Robinhood, which pioneered commission-free trading. Retail investor participation on such apps grew to almost 10 times the volume of traditional discount brokers during the 2020-2021 pandemic. Short termed trading by retail investors on platforms like Robinhood was fuelled by social networking sites such as Twitter, Discord and Reddit. These online communities allowed investors to swap stock ideas and information. Over time the communities began to have increased influence on the markets, including forcing large institutions to cover shorts after a retail investment community cooperatively targeted highly shorted securities.

Jason Goepfert is founder of Sundial Capital and SentimenTrader was kind enough to grant me an interview for this book. I wanted his perspective on the changing dynamics within this new investment climate.

As a bit of background, Jason Goepfert focuses on behavioural finance studies to manage risk. As a subscriber to Jasons work for many years, I have come to appreciate the academic rigour that he applies to all of his analysis. To put it bluntly, this man is one smart cookie. Jason has been credited for advances in the field of behavioural finance in a number of published books, academic journals and news media. In 2004, the Market Technicians Association awarded him with the very prestigious Charles H. Dow Award for excellence in the field of technical analysis and behavioural finance.

Jason notes on his website that his companies focus is "not market timing per se, but risk management. That may be a distinction without a difference, but it's how we approach the markets. We study signs that suggest it is time to raise or lower market exposure as a function of risk relative to probable reward. It is all about risk-adjusted expectations given existing evidence."

I asked **Jason Goepfert** to comment on this ever-changing investment climate, and how it might be affecting the interpretation and, indeed, the usefulness of contrarian investment tools.

Jason notes that the last decade has seen several periods where we entered "creeper" trends where historical analytical tools offer less insight as to buying or selling signals. These creeper trends seemed like permanent changes to market dynamics that wouldn't end. Until they did. When such periods ended, some or all of those gains were quickly given back. Examples of creeper trends may include the runaway FAANG bull market of the mid 2010-2020 era, Tesla's expanding valuation multiples in 2020, clean energy stocks in the 2019-2021 era, marijuana, Bitcoin and many others. Jason noted:

> "I've read various theories about why this could be, anything from belief in a Fed backstop, to a new generation of investors (like the social media investor groups discussed above) that don't have the same hang-ups as more experienced investors. I don't know the reason, and I don't know if it will continue or if it's just one of those things that happen from time to time."

Whatever the case, Jason thinks that it's more important to look at relative extremes instead of absolute ones to trade within these creeper trending environments. For example, he recommends reviewing the more recent range boundaries of an indicator versus just looking at its absolute level from an historic perspective. "That helps adjust for changes in market structure," he suggests.

One example of such a change towards using relative extremes that I have noticed can be the use of options indicators such as the VIX indicator. That's the sentiment investment **TOOL #7** discussed earlier in this chapter. My historic signal point for a "complacent" market has been at or below 12 on the VIX indicator. The realization of a move below 12 on the VIX was historically a pretty good sell signal on the S&P 500.

During 2020 & 2021, markets were trading much more aggressively than they had in the past. The rise of momentum trading shortened the timeframe and reduced the extent that a market would sell off. The VIX began to trade in a much more contained manner than my historic buy/ sell zones. I adjusted my trading to incorporate increased cash levels in the ValueTrend Equity Platform when it reached 21. You'll note in the VIX chart below that I've drawn a horizontal line near 20. That level, at least over the period noted, became a new point of investor complacency. Has the VIX found a new range to which we should adjust our buy and sell signals? To answer that, I will reference Jason's comment from above. "I don't know if it will continue or if it's just one of those things that happen from time to time." The point being, it can be useful to adjust your parameters for any indicator to fit the current environment.

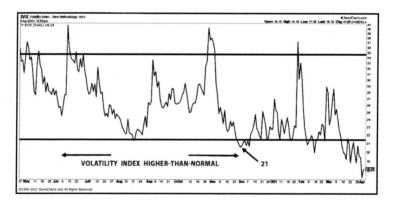

Figure 16: StockCharts — Volatility Index chart (VIX) Near termed view. Note how the VIX maintained a higher-than-normal level from mid-2020 and into 2021. As such, it became predictive that markets were reaching levels of complacency when the VIX reached around 21, as opposed to its longer termed tendency to reach complacency when the VIX approached 12 as seen in Figure 10.

KEITH G. RICHARDS

I asked Jason what new tools might become accessible to small managers and retail investors in the future though services like SentimenTrader. Jason notes that the biggest advancement for retail investors will be the availability of back-testing. As an aside, I note that back-testing sometimes gets a bad reputation. Inexperienced investors will often review an indicator over a given time period, and optimize its parameters for that time period to provide buy and sell signals. I illustrated a good example of such optimization when I noted my observations surrounding the new level for VIX buy signals during 2020/2021. An inexperienced investor might invoke some trading rules based on the results from the relatively short time horizon studied. Should the market structure change, the investor using this indicator may find that their buy or sell trigger levels become inaccurate. As you become a more experienced investor, you will develop the insight to observe when the new parameters are reverting to the traditional VIX levels. Nonetheless, Jason notes that "never before has the average investor had access to easy-to-use tools to S/B objectively test price patterns, technical indicators, or pretty much anything else. There are many software packages or sites that allow a user to test the effectiveness of a strategy, and we don't have to laboriously use Excel any longer. That should help bring more discipline and less subjectivity to forming strategies. There will always be a place for experience and gut feel, but it helps when you can clearly present historical base rates based on various criteria."

As a parting question in our conversation, I asked Jason to name his favourite indictors. In other words, if he had to live and die by his own trading success (medium term, months, not daily trading), which of the tools available to contrarian investors would he use consistently?

Jason replied that he would pick the action of retail options traders. Some of the tools from his website that incorporate this data such as **TOOL #9**, The Smart Money/Dumb Money Indicator, are incorporating this data. You can also access the options trading data directly yourself via the Options Clearing Corporations. "Retail options data allows us to see on a weekly basis who is doing what, and has proved consistently valuable over the years," says Jason.

Jason, like myself, also likes to utilize the percentage of stocks above their 200-day moving averages indicator, as useful both for determining the health of the market environment, and also for identifying potential extremes. I discuss how to interpret this indicator in the next chapter (Breadth **TOOL #2**, Non-Traditional Sentiment Indicators).

Finally, he also likes to incorporate a few traditional tools from Technical Analysis bag. He finds that the McClellan Oscillator and Summation Index indicators provide a good overview of the health and momentum underlying various indexes. While these indicators are not traditional sentiment indicators, these market breadth indicators can provide advanced clues to changes in market trends when they diverge in their direction from the US stock market indices.

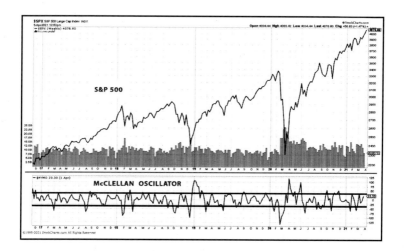

Figure 17: StockCharts — S&P 500 vs the McClellan Oscillator (bottom pane). This breadth indicator is derived from Net Advances (the number of advancing issues less the number of declining issues). Subtracting the 39-day exponential moving average of Net Advances from the 19-day exponential moving average of Net Advances forms the oscillator. The McClellan Oscillator is a momentum indicator that works similar to MACD, although the MACD is based on price activity, not breadth. I've marked horizontal lines on the oscillator at +35 and -35 to indicate potential overbought and oversold market levels.

Finally, Jason has found when Wall Street analysts upgrade (or downgrade) their price targets on a large number of stocks; it has been a consistently useful contrary indicator. There are websites out there that track these changes, including Marketwatch.com and Marketbeat.com. It's a bit time consuming to manage this data on your own, but for the ambitious investor with time on their hands, it can be done. Subscribers to SentimenTrader receive occasional tradable commentary surrounding analyst upgrades and downgrade trends via their daily emailed research pieces.

KEITH G. RICHARDS

As for the future of sentiment tools, Jason's partner Eric Brown, who holds a doctorate in Information Science, has been working on using machine learning to sort through the various sentiment and indicators and models available to investors. They are attempting to aggregate theses indicators to avoid overlapping, and add to their usefulness. The end goal is to provide access to the most valuable and reliable indicators for trading success.

BROOKE THACKRAY on Using Seasonal Cycles to Get Ahead of the Crowd ...

I asked my good friend Brooke Thackray, an acknowledged leader in the field of seasonal investing, to provide some insight into how seasonal investing can be used as a contrarian investment strategy. I first met Brooke in the early 2000s. I had read his first book, *Time In, Time Out: Outsmart the Market Using Calendar Investment Strategies*. Having just been through the devastation of the 2000 technology crash, I was searching for an answer to avoid the portfolio damage I had incurred in that meltdown. Brooke's book was a beacon of light that helped me formulate what later became my ValueTrend Investment strategy. I incorporated the "Best Six Months" seasonal strategy that Brooke outlined in his book into my investment process. In fact, I wrote about his strategy in a one of my regular columns for an investment publication. Brooke caught wind of my mentioning his book, and he contacted me. We've regularly met to discuss technical analysis and seasonal strategies since those early days.

I first started using the Best-Six-Months strategy in the early 2000s. I traded the worlds first ETF, Canada's own TSX-60 ETF known as "TIP's"(originally launched in 1990). That ETF, which mimics the TSX 60 index, is now traded under the symbol "XIU" through iShares Canada. I would buy the ETF every November and sell it in May, as outlined in Brooke's book. I eventually began to apply the Best-Six-Months strategy to the US markets by using a product mimicking the Dow Industrial Average. My vehicle of choice was the State Street Global Advisors' DIAMONDS ETF (DIA), mimicking the Dow Jones Industrial Average. That ETF was originally launched in 1993.

To this day, I continue to incorporate the influence of seasonal trends within my contrarian investment tools. In fact, you will later learn how I incorporate seasonal influence into a risk-assessment tool called the

"Bear-o-Meter." You will hear about the Bear-o-Meter in the final chapter of this book. The-Best-Six-Months strategy, along with the more sophisticated seasonal strategies outlined in Brooke's yearly investment guides are an integral part of my contrarian investment strategy. I highly recommend investors interested in contrarian investing become familiar with seasonal strategies by reading Thackray's Investors Guides.

A bit of background on Brooke Thackray: Brooke is currently a Research Analyst with Horizons ETFs (Canada) Inc. He is also President of Alpha Mountain Investments, a firm that publishes investment reports and books.

His strategies have been featured in newspapers and magazines, and he is regularly interviewed by the financial media for his expertise in seasonal and technical analysis. The following write up by Brooke Thackray will introduce you to how he incorporates seasonal investing as a contrarian investment strategy. Brooke also offers insight into some of his new work, which attempts to adjust seasonal strategies to economic policies such as federal monetary policy.

Seasonal investing is a methodology of investing that strives to take advantage of the seasonal trends of different investment assets classes, including the stock market, sectors of the stock market, commodities, bonds, and currencies. Seasonal trends exist in the market because of some underlying annual recurring causal factor that tends to increase the probability that an investment will perform well at a certain time of the year. For example, on average over the long term, the energy sector has performed well from late February into early May. In late winter and early spring, an increasing number of oil refineries shut-down for maintenance and to switch over from winter gas production to summer gas production. The oil refineries take these actions to prepare for the upcoming busy driving season that starts in May. The result is that oil and energy stocks tend to perform well heading into the driving season.

The reason that seasonal investing has been able to give investors an edge in the stock market over the long-term is not based upon the actual event occurring, but rather investor reaction in *anticipating* the event. Seasonal investing is a form of behavioural investing that is based upon the premise that it is advantageous to get into a seasonal investment before other investors and exit after other investors have pushed up the price in anticipation of a seasonal event occurring. In the example of the energy sector performing well from late February to early May, the spike in demand for oil and gasoline occurs in May. Most investors increase their investment in the sector as the demand for oil and gasoline starts to increase in May. Seasonal investors seek to enter the sector early, benefit from the increasing interest in the energy sector and exit when interest in the sector is peaking in May.

By its very nature, seasonal investing is a contrarian investment methodology. It is not a "follow the herd" methodology. Instead, it is based upon the premise of leading the herd; being there before it arrives and slipping out once it arrives. Sometimes it can be lonely entering into an investment that is starting its seasonal period and other investors have not put the investment on their radar. Successful investment strategies such as seasonal investing are akin to playing a team sport such as soccer, basketball, or hockey. The best players do not position themselves on the playing surface according to what is taking place, but rather what *will* take place.

The danger with some contrarian strategies is that they are committed to a certain investment style such as value investing. Value investing attempts to uncover overlooked stocks through fundamental analysis of factors such as book value or price to earnings ratios. For example, if the value-investment style is out of favour for an extended period, this contrarian approach can produce long-term underperformance. Seasonal investing is a unique contrarian methodology. It is not committed to a set investment style, and it is not focused on any part of the market. Sometimes it focuses on the growth sector, other times value, other times momentum and other times a variety of different sectors of the market. Seasonal investing does not marry itself to any one part of the market or to any particular investment style.

Being a contrarian investor can be an emotional experience when the dialogue in the media focuses on a crowded trade in the stock market. Letting emotions impact investment decisions is typically not a good idea. Seasonal investing has pre-established entry and exit dates that can be fine tuned with the use of technical analysis. Depending on the market cycle at any one time, a seasonal investment could line up with a popular trade with the investor crowd, or it could line up with a sector of the market that has very little interest from investors. Knowing that a seasonal trade has a finite exit point, give or take a few weeks, helps to remove the possibility of emotional attachment in making an investment decision.

Although underlying factors causing seasonal trends in the markets may not change, markets do change. What drives markets from year to year can be different. One year, the changing valuation of the US dollar may be one of the most important factors determining investment success. The next year, the shape of the yield curve on government bonds may be one of the most important factors. In recent years, central bank policy and actions have been very influential on the performance of the markets. With any investment methodology, it is important to continue to fine tune and adapt the strategy to the ever-changing markets. To sit back and believe that you have the formula set in stone to beat the markets forever is a mistake.

Investing is a journey. I constantly challenge my methodology and look for different seasonal investments, applications and changing seasonal patterns. The challenge is not to just make sure seasonal strategies that I have developed still stand, but also to look for something new, for an additional edge in the markets. Every year I write a new version of the *Thackray's Investor's Guide*. Although some of the material is updated from previous years, I challenge myself to find and include new seasonal strategies in the latest book. Although writing the book can be a difficult and demanding process, it is a valuable learning experience.

Currently, I am researching the impact of regime change on seasonal trends. Regime change is quantitative-analysis (aka "quant") language for different market conditions. For example, in an economy that is expanding faster than average, to what degree are the different seasonal cycles of the cyclical sectors of the stock market impacted? Do the entry and exit dates shift? Is it better to stay in the seasonal trade longer? Another example: In a falling interest rate environment, to what degree is the performance of the growth sector impacted and how can this be used to change the entry and exit dates?

On a prima facie basis, it appears that falling interest rates helps to provide an environment where growth stocks tend to outperform value stocks, but there are many questions to answer. For example: how much of a decline and how fast of a decline in interest rates is needed to have a meaningful impact on the relative performance of growth stocks? It is not just figuring out the relative performance of growth stocks versus the market, but also how this connects with seasonal trends.

The investment world is turning quant, whether investors like it or not. Establishing a rules-based methodology can provide the framework for a better seasonal investing discipline. Combining seasonal trends with a dynamic quant type of strategy can help provide an edge in the markets.

KEITH G. RICHARDS

Markets are going to change; they always have and always will. Using a seasonal investment discipline will continue to work in the future, how it is applied will help determine its success. No strategy works all the time: it is all about probabilities. Seasonal investing is a long-term discipline that can help investors increase their probability of success in the markets today and tomorrow.

CHAPTER 3

Using Non-traditional Sentiment Indicators

"I keep saying that the sexy job in the next 10 years will be statisticians, and I'm not kidding."

— Hal Varian, Chief Economist, Google

In this chapter, I'd like to take a look at some non-traditional sentiment indicators. These are indicators that don't necessarily measure the confidence levels of investors through confidence surveys, traditional trend analysis or option premiums. Instead, they provide clues of exuberance or fear through lesser-known price, trend and breadth interpretations. I'll also take a look at some new sentiment indicators that have emerged out of something called "Alternative Data." Tracking the crowd through language processing of trends on the internet and attitudes of investors via social media chatter is just one example of this new type of tracking the herd. We'll take a brief look at this new way of getting the inside scoop on investor behaviour later in this chapter.

BREADTH INDICATORS
Can Indicate Extremes in Crowd Behaviour

Perhaps you are familiar with market breadth indicators. These studies examine the number of stocks advancing relative to those that are declining on a broad stock market index like the S&P 500. When more stocks are advancing than declining within an uptrend, this indicates a healthy market. In typical downtrends, you will see more stocks declining than advancing. Breadth isn't limited to looking at the number of advancing vs. declining stocks on an index. Some breadth indicators, as we will examine below, compare the number of stocks within an index that are putting in new highs vs. stocks putting in new lows. Market breadth can also represent the number of stocks that are above or below key moving averages. In any case, we are trying to determine if the market is being driven by broad participation, or if it's just a concentrated group of stocks that is doing all of the lifting.

I have broken the mold a bit in using breadth indicators within my arsenal of contrarian sentiment tools. Beyond the traditional usage of breadth indicators to help determine a market's "health," we can use some breadth indicators as to measure extremes in sentiment. Let's face it: success begets success. A rising market with bullish news headlines inspires stories of success, as Robert Shiller's book referenced earlier suggested. The instinct to get with the crowd and participate in a bullish market inspires more inventors to buy an ever-growing number of stocks. During the "belly" of a bull market, this growing participation by new investors who widen the breadth of rising stocks is a positive thing. But, just like traditional sentiment indicators, there comes a time when there are "too many" participants. A rabidly bullish market inspires an increasing number of quality issues to rise. Then the crowd eventually begins to drag the lower quality names along with them. Conversely, a despondently bearish market will inspire market participants to sell with abandon starting with the overbought or overvalued stocks. Following that, they work their way down the list and sell the good names too. Throwing the baby out with the bath, as some might say. When you see widespread buying or selling of the majority of stocks within a market index, you are seeing rabid crowd behaviour.

Traditional breadth indicators like the Advance/Decline line are plotted "cumulatively" by adding or subtracting the daily reading to the last reading. The result is an indicator that presents itself as a line — much like a price line for a stock or market. They are not as useful as breadth indicators that have been plotted as an oscillator. Let's examine some of the market breadth indicators that might help provide clues to turning points in market direction.

BREADTH TOOL #1: New High/Low Indicator

The net new 52-week High/Low indicator (NHNL) is a broad market breath indictor covering the New York Stock Exchange (NYSE). The indicator is created by subtracting new lows from new highs on the stocks of the NYSE. "New lows" is the number of stocks recording new 52-week lows. "New highs" is the number of stocks making new 52-week highs. There are more new highs when the indicator is positive and more new lows when the indicator is negative. Doesn't get much simpler than that, does it? We can plot daily fluctuations as a line on most charting packages such as StockCharts.com. This creates an oscillator that meanders above and below the zero line.

I have found that if the NHNL indicator gets much higher than +300 (net 300 more new highs on the NYSE vs. new lows) it indicates a frothy market. Market participants are bidding too many stocks up, which can be a sign of bull market euphoria. I use a reading of 300+ on the NHNL indicator in my "Bear-o-Meter" model as a bearish point against the model. You'll hear more about this model later in the book.

Conversely, a reading below -200 means that the NYSE saw a net 200 new lows vs. new highs. That can indicate a panicking crowd as they dispense of stocks despite the positive longer termed prospects. I use this type of low reading on the NHNL indicator as a factor suggesting an upcoming buying opportunity in my model.

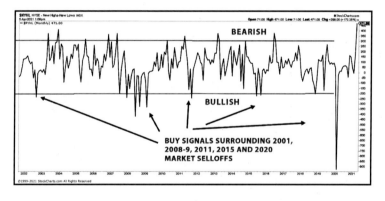

Figure 18: StockCharts — *NYSE New Highs vs. New Lows Indicator*. This indicator is particularly useful at identifying market troughs.

BREADTH TOOL #2: Percentage Stocks Over Their Moving Averages

The percentage of stocks trading above a specific moving average is a breadth indicator that measures internal strength or weakness in the underlying index.

I follow the percentage of stocks trading over their 50-day moving averages as one of the factors within my "Bear-o-Meter" risk assessment

KEITH G. RICHARDS

compilation. You'll learn more about that compilation in chapter four. The 50-day moving average version is a fairly responsive or fast moving line. As such, it can be a good near termed indicator. There are other such indicators using longer moving averages such as the percentage of stocks trading above their 150-day and 200-day moving averages on the S&P 500. Again, most of the charting packages out there offer this indicator.

Contrarian signals can be derived from overbought/oversold levels on this indicator, similar to the New High/New Low indicator shown in Figure 18. The percentage above a moving average indicator is available for many indices including the S&P 500, NASDAQ and others. I tend to focus on the S&P 500 versions, given the significance of that index to most market participants.

In my observations, if the percentage of S&P 500 stocks above the 50-day moving average gets higher than 80 (meaning that 80% of stocks in the index are above their 50-day simple moving average), it can indicate a frothy market. Market participants are bidding too many stocks up above this relatively shorter termed moving average. This can be a sign of bull market euphoria. I use this reading of 80% or higher in my "Bear-o-Meter" model. Again, the Bear-o-Meter will be discussed in the final chapter of this book.

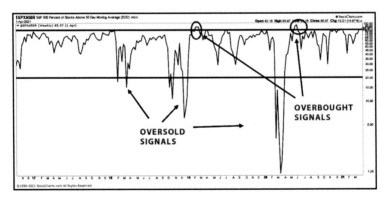

Figure 19: StockCharts — *S&P 500% of Stocks over their 50-day moving averages.* Like the New High/New Low indicator, it's most useful at identifying market troughs.

Conversely, a reading below 20% means that market participants are unwilling to bid stocks up. The S&P 500 index has only 20% of its stocks above their 50-day moving averages. Such a low reading suggests a deep level of pessimism by market participants. Too many stocks are depressed in price. Extremes in market participation — whether via high stock prices, or low prices, are unsustainable. I use a low reading on the percentage of S&P 500 stocks over their 50-day SMA's as a factor suggesting an upcoming buying opportunity in my Bear-o-Meter model.

State Street's Investor Confidence Index

I've copied the description of the State Street Investor Confidence Index directly off of their webpage, which can be found at www.statestreet.com. State Street's Investment Confidence Index differs from other sentiment indicators in that it measures sophisticated investor sentiment ("Smart Money") as a contrarian indicator. Effectively, State Street seems to treat traditional "Smart Money" as "Dumb Money" in their way of viewing contrarian trading signals. This is intriguing, given recent trends towards small investor empowerment as discussed in my interview with Jason Goepfert of SentimenTrader in chapter two.

"State Street's approach measures confidence directly and quantitatively by assessing the changes in investor holdings of risky assets. The idea is simple: the more of their portfolios that sophisticated investors are willing to devote to riskier as opposed to safer investments, the greater their risk appetite or confidence. When risk appetite increases, investors move to increase, in the same proportion, their holdings of each risky investment. This process may occur when there is good news and prices are up, but could also happen over a period of bad news and falling prices. As a result, the risk appetite of institutional investors is a separate and distinct measure from the behaviour of prices. Actual investor holdings and recent purchases provide a solid foundation on which to base a measure of investor confidence."

State Street's index hasn't been around for too long. Its data only goes back to 2012. Clearly, eight years of monthly data is not enough to draw accurate conclusions from, nor offer accurate trading signals for contrarian investing. Over time the company might have enough data to formulate some sort of leading or coincidental pattern between the index and stock market performance. In the meantime, it might be worth watching to see what happens when the indicator suggests extreme levels in confidence by sophisticated investors. Anecdotally, it appears that readings above 120 on the index could hint at an overbought market, while readings below 75 might coincide with an oversold market.

KEITH G. RICHARDS

In September of 2014, the index reached 123.9 — the highest reading that year. This corresponded to a 9% drop in the S&P 500 between September and mid-October.

Similarly, in June of 2015, the index hit 127.1, and the S&P 500 declined more than 14% between July and mid-August.

In 2019, the index stayed well below 75 (between 69.4 in January and 72.9 in April) after a 20% correction on the S&P 500 in the final quarter of 2018. That low reading on the index coincided with the start of a major S&P 500 advance.

Similarly, the State Side index fell to 73.7 during the COVID crash in March of 2020. The index declined further to 73, remaining there until May of that year. Once again, that low reading on the index coincided with the start of a major S&P 500 advance through 2020.

To reiterate, this is a relatively new sentiment indicator that you don't want to place too much confidence in. But the company has put together what appears to be an interesting confidence index that bears watching. I'd encourage you to visit their website and learn more about the index. At the time of writing this book, the index's data is available free on the website.

Historical Data

Calculations of past values for the State Street Investor Confidence Index are as follows:

	2012	2013	2014	2015	2016	2017	2018	2019	2020	2021
January	92.6	86.1	114.3	106.6	108.7	94.5	103.0	69.4	75.4	100.8
February	86.6	91.4	122.7	105.0	106.6	91.2	107.1	70.9	77.9	91.9
March	91.6	88.1	120.3	116.6	114.8	96.9	111.5	71.2	73.7	
April	87.1	93.0	119.0	113.8	108.6	97.4	115.3	72.9	73.0	
May	86.5	94.9	118.6	121.4	106.0	102.6	103.8	79.4	73.0	
June	93.3	106.8	119.3	127.1	105.7	101.0	100.8	87.3	94.0	
July	94.3	107.7	115.6	113.2	98.0	108.9	101.7	84.6	84.6	
August	91.0	104.9	120.1	109.4	89.7	106.8	94.0	76.8	86.1	
September	87.3	101.3	123.9	116.6	95.5	104.4	87.8	80.1	83.9	
October	81.2	95.5	115.8	114.0	99.2	98.1	84.4	79.2	80.1	
November	80.5	91.2	113.7	107.3	97.6	96.3	82.6	81.0	90.8	
December	81.4	95.8	112.2	110.5	94.1	95.7	79.6	79.7	104.5	

Figure 20: Statestreet's Investor Confidence Index: Historic data to March 2021

Social Media Sentiment

I'll admit that I am a social media neophyte, despite the fact that most forms of social media have been around for many years. Social media platforms such as Facebook, Instagram and Twitter have been used around the world by individuals of all ages in all walks of life. Everyone but me, it seems. Actually, to be completely honest, I do use Twitter to notify followers of my technical analysis blog updates. But I've avoided the other social platforms. Call me anti-social. Interestingly, Twitter is the subject of this section covering non-traditional contrarian indictors.

Social Sentiment as a contrarian investment tool is derived from performing automated natural language processing on messages collected from Twitter. Twitter is a micro blogging and social networking service where users can post and interact with messages. Literally hundreds of millions of people interact regularly on Twitter, offering an ideal hunting ground for those of us interesting in crowd behaviour patterns.

Companies like SentimenTrader utilize key word data coming from these interactions on Twitter. The data is categorized to determine if the crowd is Tweeting bullishly or bearishly on a market, index or stock. Messages that mention a symbol are collected and analyzed and given a rating of "bullish," "bearish" or "neutral" while negating messages categorized as "spam."

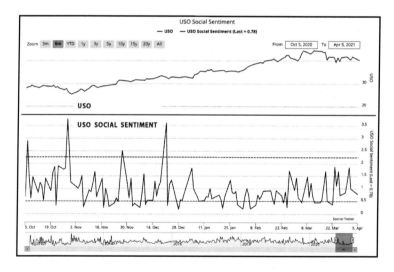

Figure 21: SentimenTrader *Social Sentiment USO (United States Oil Fund) chart.* Note how extreme pessimism on social sentiment does tend to highlight minor peaks and troughs in this oil-tracking ETF.

The ratio of bearish messages to bullish messages creates SentimenTrader's social sentiment indicator. Only premium members of

SentimenTrader can access their Social Media indicators, which track a wide range of popular index-tracking ETF's. Through SentimenTrader's indicators, you can identify contrarian signals by observing Twitter users' most hated stocks and sectors for potential contrarian buying opportunities. Conversely, you can look for stocks and sectors most loved by Twitter users as potentially overbought sell candidates.

One company that offers an interesting combination of traditional news media and social media sentiment data and analytics is Marketpsych (www.marketpsych.com). While their service is primarily aimed at institutional investors (in other words, it ain't cheap), they do offer a pretty cool summary of their data as applied to the S&P 500 on their home page. It's worth taking a look.

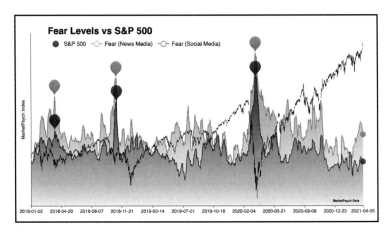

Figure 22: MarketPsych's Social media fear levels chart, with highlighted peak fear readings

Alternative Data

A pioneer in the Alternative Data field is RS Metrics. The company is a satellite imagery firm founded by Tom & Alex Diamond. UC Berkeley studied the firms retail parking lot data: They used satellite imagery to conduct daily car counts conducted from 2011 to 2017 at 67,000 stores representing 44 major US retailers including Costco, Nordstrom, Starbucks, Target, Walmart, Whole Foods and others. The parking lots are monitored by satellites for car-counts, and look for anomalies in these counts during comparable dates and hours.

It was found that if you had bought shares of retailers when parking-lot traffic patterns increased abnormally and sold its shares when it declined, you would have earned a return that was 4.7% higher than simply buying and holding the same stock over comparable periods. More cars in parking lots mean higher earnings, leading to higher stock prices.

There are many other types of Alternative Data being used by investment analysts, hedge funds and institutional investors. Alternative Data can scan geolocations to identify where individual computing devices are being used and its surrounding online browsing activity. It looks for consumer and corporate Internet search and usage patterns that might signal market opportunities, or risk. It looks at corporate hiring activity, corporate FX activity and other atypical metrics to find an edge in identifying future stock performance.

Companies like S&P Global Marketplace catalogues various data sets, which, for a price, is accessible to sophisticated investment firms. Of interest to contrarian investors is their usage of "Textual Data." This service extracts key words and phrases using "Natural Language Processing" (NLP) to analyze sentiment and transparency on 10,000 companies throughout the world. They provide text analysis algorithms summarizing articles, commentaries, public filings, earnings transcripts, and research opinions through meta data tagging. I discussed one type of NLP data mining on page 65 where I covered social sentiment indicators.

Bloomberg Professional Services offers an array of Alternative Data for institutional investors and sophisticated traders. App downloads and usage, corporate flight activity, employee and customer satisfaction via social media verbiage (NLP) data is available. Bloomberg examines various sources to locate rumours of events such as mergers and acquisitions, patents, and ESG (environmental, social, governance) optics. Bloomberg also sells data that tracks and predicts consumer purchasing, spending trends, and even medical prescription data. Like S&P Global MarketPlace, they monitor corporate news sentiment, website, television and media language. Mind boggling stuff!

While much of this Alternative Data is too costly to be accessible to most retail investors and small portfolio managers, take heart! Companies like S&P, Bloomberg, Thomson Reuters and others are starting to offer lower priced packages. Serious investors like you and I will soon be able to afford their services. Keep an eye on the websites of these firms for oncoming retail investor products and services in the Alternative Data arena.

KEITH G. RICHARDS

GOOGLE TRENDS

In the past, we relied on surveys and polling to uncover clues surrounding everything from potential political outcomes to consumer habits. Of course, polls and surveys only reach a small sampling of the population. Moreover, individuals who are surveyed are not always willing to disclose the truth. In other words, surveys can be pretty misleading.

Enter Google Trends. According to Alternative Data research service Arbar Data Services, 59% of the entire world uses the Internet. Moreover, the developed world usage of Internet is almost unilateral amongst its population. Some 4.5 billion people across the globe search the Internet using Google. Google trends tracks Internet search patterns over a vast number of topics. Google Trends categorize search topics under something near 140 broad categories. These categories are further broken down into sub topics (e.g., inflation, gold, travel, etc) and then further again into specific search terms.

Unlike surveys of the past, Google Trends looks at real data in these categories and search patterns over a massive population. Internet searchers may lie to a survey company, but their actions speak louder than their words when we track their actual search enquiries. How will this data help us as contrarian investors? Investors willing to do a little digging can use Google Trends to uncover accurate and timely trends surrounding investment sentiment. We can track the trend, and the declining interest in an investment theme by monitoring investment categories of interest on Google Trends. By doing this, we can get a heads up on emerging trends, or declining interest in many investment categories. The great news is that Google Trends is free! It's available to all of us, and can help us discover contrarian sentiment opportunities.

According to Benjamin Breitholtz, data scientist at Arbar Data Services, investors who examine Google search activity data need to take three steps when analyzing Google Trends:

1. **Trend recognition — Is there a clear and obvious growing trend of Google search activity in the category you are researching?**

2. **Seasonality — When noting a trend, adjust for seasonal norms. For example, travel and leisure searches are more prevalent during key periods of the year. Using seasonal patterns from sources like Brooke Thackray's books (see my interview with Brooke Thackray in the last chapter) can help with this type of filters**

3. Shock — Sometimes a quick spike in an internet search on a security can alert us to a contrarian trade. Investors are often myopic, quickly willing to move on after a short spurt in interest. For example, let's say you own gold. Google Trends shows a sudden interest in the gold trade as the price spikes. Perhaps it's now best to keep a sharp eye on your gold position. Prices can fall quickly if the herd decides to lose interest in the investment. With search "shocks," the herd can lose interest as quickly as it became interested in something.

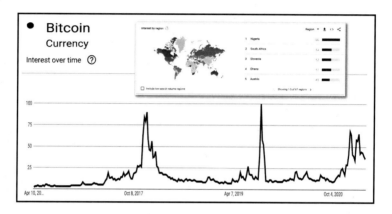

Figure 23(A): Bitcoin chart from Google Trends March 2016 – March 2021. The line represents search interest relative to the highest point on the chart for worldwide searches under the term "Bitcoin" during this timeframe. A value of 100 is the peak popularity for the term. A value of 50 means that the term is half as popular. Peak interest occurred in the week of December 17-23 2017, and the week of September 1-7 2019. Bitcoin searches also spiked during the week of January 3-9 and Feb 21-27 in 2021.

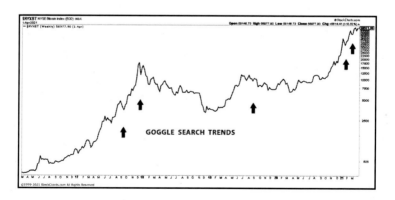

Figure 23(B): StockCharts — NYSE Bitcoin index March 2016 – March 21st. Arrows note the Google trends search peaks noted in Figure 22(A). There are indications that peak Google searches in Bitcoin and other "hot" investments coincide roughly with price peaks in the security.

I began exploring Google Trends to spot potentially emerging positive investor sentiment in sectors with bullish chart patterns. A technical breakout on a chart backed by a pattern of increased Google searches can indicate upside potential in that security. Conversely, sudden spikes or "shocks" in search behaviour can provide contrarian alerts. Figure 23(A) illustrates a Google Trends chart illustrating searches of the word "Bitcoin." You can spot contrarian sell signals on the chart when search activity spiked on Bitcoin enquiries. The Bitcoin index chart seen in Figure 23(B) illustrates how prices peaked on the Bitcoin index precisely in-line with Google search enquiry peaks. I'd encourage you to explore the Google Trends site yourself to enhance your investment intel when reviewing existing or potential new investment candidates. Or, you can subscribe to services by companies like Arbar Data Science to filter Google search data using their sophisticated criteria to discover emerging investment opportunities.

Combining Contrarian Models with Political Analysis: An interview with **Larry McDonald** of BearTraps …

Lawrence "Larry" G. McDonald is a *New York Times* bestselling author and CNBC contributor, and the founder of Beartraps, which is a research service focused on Political and Systemic Risk and Macro perspective. He was former Head of US Macro Strategy at Societe Generale, but he is best known for his world-leading investment performance in distress debt and convertible securities trading at Lehman Brothers. I have been a subscriber to his institution-level research for a few years, and feel that it is amongst the single most valuable source of contrarian investment themes I have ever run across. Larry combines the use of traditional sentiment work with a very interesting type Alternative Data to identify investment opportunities. He was kind enough to provide some insight into this unique contrarian model.

During his tenure at Lehman Brothers, Larry developed a series of factors to help him identify opportunistic buying or selling opportunities within distressed debt securities. In addition to the individual security analysis utilized by Larry and his team, a compilation of 21 Lehman Systemic Indicators were adapted to measure macro (broad market) risk vs. reward profiles.

A number of the Lehaman Indicators, along with new inputs he incorporated over the years, became his "Capitulation Model." The idea behind this model is to measure human psychology, with a particular emphasis on identifying periods of maximum pessimism during market selloff situations. To quote Larry, "We're looking to find those moments where there's no sellers left." His model attempts to classify the relative degree of a market capitulation, much like environmental engineers might classify a hurricane for its strength. Hurricanes are typically classified on a scale of one-to-five, where five holds the greatest potential strength.

Larry's financial capitulation model is a mathematical probability model designed to determine the potential success on buying opportunistically into a major selloff. Similar to the hurricane model, his capitulation model classifies the potential strength of a market move on a scale ranging from a strong opportunity to a lesser one. Opportunities are ranked according to the degree of pessimism and price capitulation. In this way, the model helps him estimate potential upside for taking a contrarian trade.

While the "formula" for his model remain proprietary to BearTraps, Larry was kind enough to provide an outline of some of the factors he looks at. It should be noted that many of the tools below are discussed in the previous chapter of this book. The BearTraps capitulation model includes:

- **The discounts that ETF's (Exchange Traded Funds) are trading at vs. their current NAV's (Net Asset Values).**

- **A money flow model tracking the total net shares into an asset vs. out of an asset.**

- **The distance below the lower Bollinger Band that the price of a security has moved to.** (*A Bollinger Band is a technical analysis tool defined by a set of lines plotted two standard deviations [positively and negatively] away from a simple moving average [SMA] of the security's price.*)

- **The breadth of selling within a market or sector.**

KEITH G. RICHARDS

Larry has found that the occurrence of two capitulation signals triggered within about six months — aided by a political event catalyst — can lead into the " *greatest trading opportunities in one's trading career.*" Herein lies the real value of a service like BearTraps. As with many of the Alternative Data tools discussed above, access to political data is a key differentiator for Larry's model. As Larry notes, "Everyone has access to data, which is great ... but to outperform in the current market, you need to have that extra step for an edge." Political analysts ACG Analytics is in partnership with BearTraps. Larry uses their high-level political survey and policy interpretation research to add the Alternative Data edge for BearTrap's investment success. The company analyses specific policy issues and actions in the United States, the European Union, Asia and Latin America. Their research anticipates how government policies in key markets may impact investor strategies. BearTraps attempts to incorporate a political model provided by AGC's research, and combine the key predictions from that model with their own capitulation model. This alternative research data increases the potential for a positive outcome on a contrarian investment theme.

Interestingly, as I was writing this book during the latter half of 2020, BearTraps had identified one of those "greatest trading opportunity" setups. That is, two subsequent signals coming out of the BearTraps capitulation model that occur within 6 months, combined with a key political event.

During the initial part of 2020, crude oil inventories were building in the US and abroad. The worldwide economic shutdowns imposed by countries attempting to combat the novel COVID virus pandemic drove consumption of energy products to a near standstill. Reports of oil tankers and storage facilities reaching maximum capacity were circulating. WTIC crude had been trading in the mid-$60's at the start of the year, then plummeted to $20 during the height of the CIVID-inspired market crash. Then came the panic.

Fearing the failure to coordinate a slowing of production as storage facilities neared peak capacity; traders evacuated their positions. It was conceivable that the cost of storing oil would outweigh the value of the product. Traders holding oil would potentially experience both capital losses AND would be on the hook for storage costs. On April 20, 2020, the US benchmark price for crude dropped below zero for the first time — and then kept falling. The future contracts for May delivery of West Texas

Intermediate tumbled to *minus* $37.63 a barrel! Without a doubt, says Larry, this event was one of the most important events in world history.

The BearTraps' capitulation model identified an opportunity. Potential US shale producer lobbying along with observations of high-level political discussions within oil producing countries were observed by AGC Analytics. The combination of capitulating investor behaviour in conjunction with a significant political catalyst inspired the equivalent of a "level 5 hurricane" within the BearTraps model. The production cuts by Saudi Arabia and Russia had underestimated future consumption trends. Oil began to rise again, moving back to the low-$40's by the summer.

Just when things seemed to be getting back on track for oil prices, things began to look grim again for energy traders. In late November 2020, a second capitulation signal occurred on the BearTraps model. The "Biden Blue Wave" political movement had begun, to take hold. Then-candidate Biden was known to be less supportive to fossil fuel energy producers. There was a genuine concern by the industry surrounding the potential of his bid towards the presidency. Biden was campaigning on the new "Green Movement" towards solar, EV's and carbon reduction. The election was going to a close one, and energy producers in the USA were in full panic mode. Traders joined the panic. The combination of these two events created a plethora of sellers across the market in November. Oil prices were chopped by approximately 25%, retreating into the low-$30's.

All the energy space needed was a catalyst to move higher. That catalyst appeared as talks of the COVID vaccination accelerated alongside an increasing realization of Saudi Arabia's overestimation in the amount of cuts needed. Traders had also miscalculated the growing consumption of fossil fuel products in the world's fastest growing countries — China and India. The political Intel provided by AGC examined movements around Capital Hill and Saudi Arabia. The BearTraps capitulation model, along with international oil consumption patterns and political intelligence on influences and policy changes predicted an opportunity. BearTraps recommended buying the energy producers when everyone else was selling. This, again, turned out to be Larry's second outstanding contrarian call on oil for the year. Crude oil moved from $33 in mid November to over $50/barrel by the year-end. When I interviewed Larry in late January 2021, BearTraps was still bullish on the oil trade.

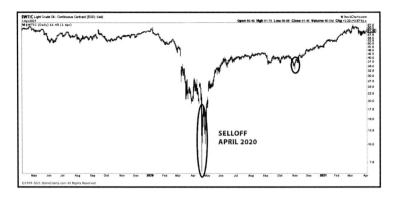

Figure 24: StockCharts — Light Sweet crude oil ($WTIC) illustrating the April 2020, capitulation and the November 2020 lesser selloff.

I'd like to note that I am not associated with BearTraps in any way other than as a subscriber. I do recommend that if you are a larger investor, it may be worth exploring BearTraps to see if it could add value to your investment strategy. The Beartraps Report is actually very affordable for most small to mid sized Portfolio Management firms and individual investors with larger portfolios. Beartraps research is available for about $3000 USD per year. In my mind, such a service could more than offset its price if the cost works out to be about 1% of your total portfolios value. Ultimately, any expenses taken on by an investor that might offer a greater percentage upside than the cost of the research has to be considered. Services like BearTraps may have the potential to add that upside to your returns.

CHAPTER 4

Putting It All Together — 3 STEPS to Portfolio Happiness

"You can't predict. You can prepare."

— Howard Marks,

Co-Chairman Oaktree Capital Management

My firm, ValueTrend Wealth Management, provides clients with an acceptable rate of return with as little risk as possible. Like I mentioned in the opening chapter of this book, I learned the hard way about risk when I lost big in the 2001 technology crash. Limiting risk became a cornerstone of the investment philosophy surrounding ValueTrend's investment strategies. A big part of controlling portfolio risk at ValueTrend has been successfully incorporating many of the sentiment tools discussed in this book.

In this chapter, I'd like to take a look at the specific contrarian and sentiment indicators that I typically use in in my practice as Technical Analyst and Chief Portfolio Manager for ValueTrend. By discussing the tools I use in managing real money for real clients, this book offers a more hard-nosed and practical guide to investing than the conceptual approach taught in many financial advice books. In this chapter, I hope to impart to you this pragmatic, step-by-step approach to increase your odds of a profitable, lower risk portfolio. Now, let's begin by taking a brief look at three steps you can take when formulating your investment strategy. I'll expand on these steps as we progress through this chapter.

STEP 1: Broad-Market Analysis

The first step in determining your level of commitment to the stock market, or to specific market sectors, is to employ a top-down or "macro" view of the investment climate. Phases, as discussed in my book *Sideways*, affect both the broader markets as well as the individual securities that you are studying. There are four market phases. Markets can trend *up*, or trend *down*. If they are not trending, they can *consolidate* in bottoming or topping patterns. It should be noted that markets can also consolidate for short periods of time during trending markets, but these are typically called "continuation" patterns rather than a topping or bottoming phase.

The basic idea behind identifying phases is this: A trending market can be identified by a successive series of peaks and troughs on price chart in a given direction. Observing a longer termed moving average such as the 200-day moving average can help confirm the phase.

For example, a market in an uptrend makes higher peaks and higher troughs on its weekly chart while spending the majority of the time above its 200-day moving average. Markets in a downtrend display successive lower peaks and troughs. They spend most of the time below their 200-day moving average. Stocks that are consolidating make random peaks and troughs within a consolidation pattern. The price of such stocks tends to move up and down through their 200-day moving average with no clear direction.

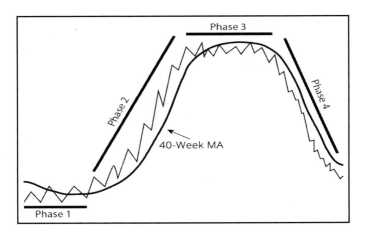

Figure 25: Phases of the market

Identify these phases to reduce your exposure to equities when the broader picture is a downtrend. Increase your exposure to equities when your analysis points to a bullish market — for example, after a identifying a breakout from a consolidation pattern or during an uptrend.

STEP 2: Confirmation

After identifying the current phase of the market as a potential buying opportunity, you will want to examine the potential longevity and strength of the market. This is done by reviewing market breadth, market sentiment, and the current value of the markets through a tool like my Bear-o-Meter compilation, which will be discussed in detail shortly.

Let's assume you are convinced that the outlook for the market is bullish. STEP 1 shows us that the trend is up. Now you want to do a deeper dive into the sustainability of that trend. Is market breadth healthy (without being overbought), illustrating strong participation by many stocks and sectors? Are your favoured sentiment indicators illustrating a healthy balance between investor optimism and caution? Where are you in the seasonal cycle of the market?

The Bear-o-Meter, described below, is my way of putting together a point system to answer those questions. It contains many of the indictors described in this book, along with a few other indicators that measure trend, seasonality, valuation and breadth. However, it doesn't contain all of the contrarian investment tools discussed in this book. It's what works for me. You might want to construct your own compilation of tools within your process. Perhaps you prefer to concentrate on long termed indicators with less emphasis on those sentiment tools that can move violently in and out of overbought or oversold conditions. In such a case, you might be less interested in using the options-based sentiment tools like the VIX or the Put/Call ratio. You might switch out the percentage of stocks over their 50-day moving average to the percentage of stocks over their 200-day moving average for a longer termed breadth-momentum indicator. The point is, STEP 1 identified that the market is in a healthy uptrend. STEP 2 is about confirming the health of that trend. You need to know if that uptrend is showing any internal cracks in the foundation. Are there signs that this bull trend is becoming too frothy? Contrarian tools are there to give you a heads up on a potentially overbought market. It can help you determine the potential longevity of the current uptrend. Conversely, it can also give you advance notice that the current downtrend may soon reverse and turn into a bullish investment opportunity.

Now that you've satisfied your parameters for the risk/reward trade-offs using your chosen sentiment indicators, the next step is to identify sectors that offer the best potential. Seasonal patterns for various sectors should be considered. Brooke Thackray's Investors Guides offer a quick and handy reference to these patterns. Trademiner.com is a cost effective seasonal trading service that scans for current seasonal opportunities on individual US stocks, futures and currencies. Scanning through SentimenTrader's sector ETF's Optix readings for favourable conditions and looking for trending or basing technical patterns on those sectors are part of this step.

From there, you will want to analyze the finer details of the patterns that you have identified. Technical Analysis tools like momentum indicators and candlestick analysis help you confirm the legitimacy of your observations; both for the broader markets and for the individual sectors and securities you plan to trade. My book *Sideways* covers many of these tools, and how to use them.

STEP 3: Risk Control

As noted in STEP 2, you want to utilize macro market risk analysis that incorporates contrarian indicators, such as my Bear-o-Meter, as part of your investment strategy. These tools don't just help you decide when to buy. They can help you decide when to sell as well.

A heads-up of growing risk provided by contrarian indicators can influence your decision to reduce equity exposure by selling stocks to raise cash. You might also choose to lower the beta of your portfolio by selling higher risk stocks and re-allocating into lower risk stocks. Beta is the measurement of a stock's volatility in relation to the overall market. The market, represented by indices like the S&P 500 Index, has a beta of 1.0. Individual stocks are ranked according to how much they deviate in volatility (up or down) from the market. A stock that swings more than the market over time has a beta above 1.0. A stock that swings less than the market has a beta below 1.0. Higher risk markets might influence you to sell high beta stocks and buy low beta stocks, even if you don't want to hold cash. That's because low beta stocks will, on average, fall less in a declining market than will stocks with market-equal or higher beta profiles.

Beyond the decision to raise cash or lower beta if risk is high, you will want to incorporate a stop-loss strategy on your individual positions. This strategy can help you remain invested while markets trend higher in an ever-growing risk environment, while knowing that you have an "insurance" policy of limiting your losses should your stocks begin to decline as market risk materializes. *Securities that are breaking down illustrate a lower low and a lower peak on a chart, and a break below the 200-day moving average.* The GE chart in Figure 26 illustrates this concept perfectly.

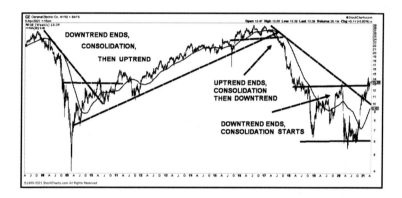

Figure 26: StockCharts — General Electric (GE-US) illustrates the 4 phases of a market cycle nicely. Note the transitions between the phases, which can be verified by noting successive levels in peaks and troughs along with confirmations by the 200-day (40 week) moving average.

Employ your sell rules on your individual sectors and stocks through trend analysis, contrarian signals and stop-loss strategies. Reduce your portfolio beta by switching into lower risk stocks or sectors upon a bearish contrarian signal. We'll review these strategies later when we get to the journey into contrarian investing of Mary Contrary.

The Bear-o-Meter Indicator

The Bear-o-Meter Indicator is a contrarian toolbox that enables us to reduce our broad equity exposure in overbought, over concentrated or irrational markets. The following is taken from a paper I wrote for the Canadian Society of Technical Analysis (CSTA) in their 2017 journal. It covers all of the indicators utilized within the Bear-o-Meter, several of which you will be familiar with from the prior chapters in this book. The paper was well received — possibly because of the humorous approach I took within a normally dry and academic atmosphere.

In the journals forward, James Ivey, past President of the CSTA, wrote this:

"The first paper is from Keith Richards, CMT, CIM, FCSI and Portfolio Manager at ValueTrend Wealth Management. In his pleasurable and witty article he guides us through the compilation and evaluation of his Bear-o-Meter indicator to assess risks and rewards in the market. Keith has a direct and funny style and you will enjoy and benefit from his wisdom packaged in this informative and highly useful article. Moreover, the indicators he describes can be used — together or in isolation — to inform your own trading and investing decisions."

I use a system that tries to identify the relative risk versus reward potential of the US markets at any given time. It incorporates 11 indicators that fall under five different categories and applies them to judging relative risk on the popular S&P 500 index. I call this collection of indicators the "Bear-o-Meter."

The Bear-o-Meter is a forward-looking risk indicator of the market. It is not a near-termed timing tool — in fact, its signals can often be one-to-three months early. As a qualifier to understand this tool, it's important to remind ourselves of the realities behind "market timing." Market timing is not about picking peaks and troughs. While sometimes we can do this with some level of accuracy, it's a bit of a mugs game to be consistently right at picking those precise pivot points. If you can accurately and unfailingly identify exact market peaks and troughs, please send me a resume with conclusive proof of that claim. Your starting salary will be $1-million.

A more realistic view of market timing might be that of identifying the current levels of risk vs. return present on the markets. Markets have risk, and have potential reward simultaneously at all times. The Bear-o-Meter simply weighs those two potentials, and tries to determine which of those two sides is skewed more heavily on the risk/reward scale.

A low reading on the Bear-o-Meter indicates bearish potential, but it does not suggest selling your portfolio out and hiding the cash under your mattress. Markets can still go up in a higher risk environment. A high Bear-o-Meter reading suggests bullish conditions, but does this not imply that you should leverage the farm to buy stocks. Markets can still fall within a lower risk environment.

All readings on the Bear-o-Meter are simply a relative reading of reward and risk potential. Again, markets always have the potential to make you poor or make you rich. They are simply skewed towards one side or the other at any given moment. As I like to point out to people who attend my talks, the stock market is like a giant casino when viewed in the near-term. The only thing that systems like my Bear-o-Meter give you is an edge within that greater unknown.

The Bear-o-Meter is a compilation of 11 indicators.

- **Two are trend indicators**
- **Four are breadth indicators (although I use two of them as momentum indicators)**
- **One is a value indicator**
- **Three are sentiment indicators**
- **One is plain old seasonality (best/worst six months)**

I always get a kick out of the players in our industry who try to make the system they follow sound exotic and unattainable by common folk. They do this by calling their system "proprietary." Seriously, folks, there's not much to be "proprietary" or "exotic" about in Technical Analysis. We deal with three not-so-exotic factors: price, volume, time (I'll leave open interest out of this group given its sole application to derivatives). That's it. All technical stock market indicators are comprised of one or more of those three factors.

Everything we use in Technical Analysis contains price, volume, and time. Even sentiment indicators measure volume (volume of bullish or bearish opinions). That means we can all look at the same stuff. Nobody has proprietary license or sole access to these three factors, and we can all find them quickly on a charting or research service to create an indicator. Moreover, most of the indicators that are created from those three factors are available on free charting services. It's how we interpret these factors that counts!

Okay, so enough of that rant. Here are the highly exotic, mysterious, never before seen indicators I use when putting together my Bear-o-Meter Indicator (tongue firmly in my cheek here, folks). Please destroy this page after reading it (Ethan Hunt, Mission Impossible).

Please note that I recommend you study each of these indicators yourself to further refine their relative measurements of risk/return potential. I'm not the all-knowing authority on these indicators. You might find more accurate levels than I use on these indicators. I encourage you to experiment and explore the concepts I've used to create the Bear-o-Meter. This isn't rocket surgery, folks. Anyone with a bit of knowledge in Technical Analysis can tweak the various signal points to meet their trading horizons or risk tolerance.

TRENDS

To analyze trend, I track the 50-day SMA and 200-day SMA showed in Figure 27 below (don't worry about the arrows for now). I note if the market (S&P 500) is above or below these indicators (Figure 27 below). If the market is above these moving averages, it is considered to be trending positively. If the market is below, the trend is negative — relatively speaking. Positive, or negative points are assigned to each depending on where the market sits relative to these SMA's. A positive reading is given to the market being above the SMA in question and a negative point is given for the market being below the SMA. Two points positive or negative are assigned to the 200-day SMA reading, and one point (positive or negative) is assigned to the 50-day SMA reading. Obviously, the relationship of price to a longer termed moving average is more significant than that of the shorter moving average.

Figure 27: StockCharts — S&P 500 with the 200-day moving average (40 week, solid line).

"I told you this wasn't rocket surgery.
Let's move on"!

— **Keith G. Richards**

BREADTH

Breadth is all about market participation — and how broad, or widespread, it is. Narrow breadth means less participation, or concentrated strength within fewer sectors or stocks. Generally speaking, a rising market should be supported by rising breadth. I use four breadth indictors within the Bear-o-Meter, although two of them are used more like momentum readings than true breadth readings. I'll explain how I interpret each indicator below:

1. My favourite breadth indicator is the cumulative Advance Decline (NYSE) line on the weekly chart (below) and look at the 40 week SMA of the AD line, and assign a positive or negative point according to whether the AD line is above or below that SMA. I also note if the AD line is diverging (Y or N) vs. the S&P 500. If it is diverging bullishly (moving opposite to the S&P500's trend) like it was in 2009, that's another positive point assigned to the Bear-o-Meter. Bearish divergence vs. the S&P 500 is a negative point. I'm effectively looking for non-confirmation of a new high or new lows on the AD line vs. the S&P 500.

Figure 28: StockCharts — The Advance / Decline Line (top line on chart) vs. the S&P 500 (bottom line on chart)

KEITH G. RICHARDS

Another breadth reading I like to take is the movement of the Dow Jones Industrials vs. the Dow Jones Transportation stocks (Figure 29 below). On StockCharts the tickers are INDU vs. TRAN. Dow Theory contains a tenet suggesting the Dow Transportation index must confirm the highs and direction of the Industrials. Despite the theory's faults (it tends to either lag or lead a correction by long time periods), the indicator has rarely missed a market correction when Transports diverge (this, according to Dow Theorists who keep long termed performance records). As with the confirmation analysis with the AD line, I'm effectively looking for non-confirmation of a new high or new lows on the INDU vs. the TRAN. I assign a neutral "0" point to the Bear-o-Meter if they are moving in tandem, and a negative point if they diverge with the TRAN failing to confirm a new peak on the INDU.

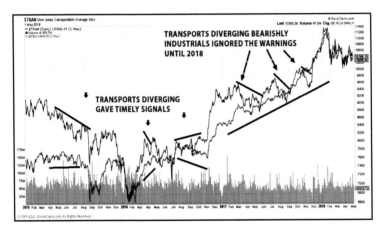

Figure 29: StockCharts — DOW INDUSTRIALS VS. DOW TRANSPORTS. This breadth indicator is typically quite accurate at predicting a change in direction for the DJIA when the transports diverge — either bullishly or bearishly. A bearish divergence occurs when the transports move down against a rising industrials index. A bullish divergence occurs when the transports move up against a falling industrial index. You'll note the accurate signals on the left side of the chart. However, in 2017 after Trump was elected, business tax cuts and easy money from the US Federal Reserve pushed the Industrials into its strongest uptrend in years. Transports didn't benefit as much as other sectors, hence the three negative divergences. Nonetheless, the DJIA (and the S&P 500) had the lowest daily volatility in their respective histories. By 2018, that excess was taken out through two significant pullbacks — suggesting that the divergences by the transports gave us accurate, if not timely signals.

I follow two other breadth indicators and assign positive or negative ratings to their readings. Technical Analysts use these indicators to look at market breadth. These indicators can also indicate overbought and oversold situations — which is how I interpret them for the purposes of the Bear-o-Meter. The first of these two indicators is the NYSE New High/New low indicator. When too many stocks on the NYSE are making new highs or above their 50-day SMA's, markets may be getting overbought. For the $NYHL indicator, I look at readings over 300 (net new highs) on this index as a negative (overbought) point, and a reading of less than 200 as a positive point (oversold market). In between those levels is a neutral condition. These indicators were discussed in Chapter Two of this book.

VALUATION

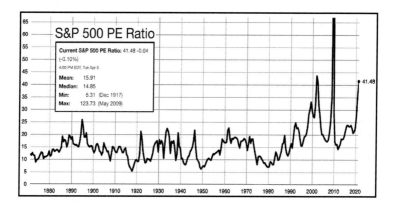

Figure 30: Multpl.com's — PE ratio chart goes back to the late 1800s. Interestingly, since 1990 the S&P 500 has seen regular levels that far exceed my threshold of 23. This has likely been due to lower interest rates, which tend to encourage business expansion and earnings growth. Unprecedented low interest rates have been making PE ratios less significant. Still, should rates rise, perhaps the PE ratio will matter more to stock investors than it does when money is easy.

PE ratio is one of those rabbit holes that simple folk like me try to avoid. First, you have to decide which type of PE ratio you are going to look at. Yes, there are lots of different PE ratio's used by fundamental analysts (just as there are lots of momentum oscillators on our side of the pond). Choose your poison: Is your favourite PE ratio based on trailing earnings? What about forward earnings? Or better still, what about Robert Shiller's CAPE (Cyclically Adjusted Price Earnings)? Further — what is an "overvalued" or "undervalued" PE level? Is this time different? What about the relationship of earnings growth to the PE? Most of these statistics are tracked on the website www.multpl.com. I use their reading of the S&P 500's trailing PE ratio.

Like I said, this is a *very* deep rabbit hole. And given that I'm a Technical Analyst, I probably shouldn't be messing with this fundamental stuff. Just like I shouldn't try to fix my own car. But I had noticed there seems to be some correlation between markets eventually peaking and toughing when the trailing PE ratio gets to certain levels. So I assign a positive point to the Bear-o-Meter if the S&P 500's trailing PE goes to 13 or below. I assign a negative point if it rises above 23. No points (neutral) are between those levels. Please don't send hate mail to me on my PE ratio interpretation. I'll not have time to read it, as I'm busy fixing my car.

SENTIMENT

"Pooh always liked a little something at eleven o'clock in the morning, and he was very glad to see Rabbit getting out the plates and mugs; and when Rabbit said, 'Honey or condensed milk with your bread?' he was so excited that he said, 'Both,' and then, so as not to seem greedy, he added, 'But don't bother about the bread, please.'"

— A. Milne (1882–1956)

If you've been following my blog at www.valuetrend.ca for a few years, or have read either of my books, you will know that I follow plenty of sentiment indicators. These indicators utilize the concept of contrary investment thinking. I've always believed that (forgive my cynicism here) the crowd, or majority of people, typically follow others mindlessly without much independent thought. This applies to most things in life. While such herd behaviour may be fine for fashion (skinny suits, no socks) or automotive choice (people who never get their hands dirty seem to love shiny pickup trucks of late), it's not so great for outperforming the stock market. You really don't want to participate when the crowd reaches high points of fear and greed.

The best way to utilize contrary thinking within the investment world is through sentiment indicators. The basic premises of sentiment indicators are that — when ill-informed investors are "too" bullish, you should start selling. If the majority of these folks are "too" bearish, back up the truck and load it up with stocks. You can also monitor the movements of groups of investors who are usually more accurate in their decisions ("Smart Money"). In fact, you can compare the activities of Smart Money to those groups who are usually lousy investment decision makers ("Dumb Money"). So, if commercial hedgers and pension fund managers are usually right — you want to follow those investors — do what they do. Conversely, you want to fade, or trade against, the decisions made by typically inaccurate retail mutual fund investors, small speculators, and small options traders. When you see the two groups in diametrically opposed trading modes, you have an even stronger signal.

Here are the three sentiment indicators that I use in the Bear-o-Meter, all of which have been discussed in chapter two of this book:

1. The Smart/Dumb Money confidence spread (SentimenTrader.com) is an indicator that I have incorporated into the Bear-o-Meter. The chart in Figure 14 on page 48 of this book shows us a spread between the two groups. It's calculated by taking the "smart" vote, and then dividing the "dumb" vote into it. It gives us a ratio of Smart : Dumb Money confidence. You will notice that the best sell signals seem to come from a deep negative spread, and the best buy signals come from a deep positive spread. Typically, we see levels of -0.50 for the best sell signals, and 0.50 for the best buy signals. Note the relatively large number of good calls that this indicator has made. But it's had some false signals (head fakes) too. I've highlighted both on the chart above. For the purpose of the Bear-o-Meter, I assign a positive point for readings on the confidence spread indicator that are above 0.25, and a negative point for readings that are below -0.25. All other readings are neutral.

2. The VIX is another sentiment indicator that is incorporated into the Bear-o-Meter. Normally, we look at VIX levels to determine how understated or overstated the implied volatility of the stock market is. The VIX provides data via the CBOE options premiums. High VIX levels — anywhere near 35 or higher — usually signal a market bottom or the end of a corrective period for stocks. That's because high VIX levels indicate capitulation and fear through overzealous volatility premiums by options traders. Such a reading gives the Bear-o-Meter a positive point. Low VIX levels — somewhere near 12 or lower — signal a

KEITH G. RICHARDS

higher probability for a market correction, or the end of a bullish period for stocks. That's because a low VIX reading indicates a certain level of complacency by options traders — and complacent is one thing you don't want to be when trading stocks. You can see these tendencies on the long termed VIX chart in Figure 10 on page 41. The VIX can remain low for many months! But it doesn't stay still forever. A reading of below 12 on the VIX gives the Bear-o-Meter a negative point.

3. The COEB total options Put/Call ratio measures the net trading activity in defensive (puts) options vs. bullish (call) options. Too many puts (compared to trading in calls) means too much pessimism — and vice versa. But only at extremes. I've drawn a line at the ratio of 1.25 puts/1 call as bearish (top line) and 0.75 puts/1 call as bullish. Please refer to the chart in Figure 9, page 41 of this book. A positive, negative, or neutral point is assigned to the Bear-o-Meter according to these levels.

SEASONALITY: Best Six Months, Worst Six Months

The concept of this strategy is to reduce equity during the May 5th-to-October 27th period, then become fully invested for the other six months. Carrying that strategy a little further, seasonal experts Jeffery Hirsch, Brooke Thackray and Don Vialoux note that certain sectors will tend to do better than others at different times of the year. For example, seasonal patterns typically suggest holding more defensive sectors such as utilities and bonds during the "worst six months" for stocks. High beta sectors like technology and consumer discretionary stocks tend to do well in the favourable six months. Obviously the seasonal strategies are not guaranteed to work each and every year for either the broad markets or sector/asset class rotation. Further, the problem with the "worst six months" (May-to-the end of October) is not so much with the frequency of pullbacks during that period. True, there is a tendency for markets to be a little weaker — if not negative — during the summer, more often than not; however, that's not the case every year. The real problem for markets is the intensity of a pullback — if one does occur during the worst six months. I don't give the summer a "negative" reading, simply because the big pullbacks don't occur regularly enough to make it a high probability event. But strong markets during the winter, on a relative basis, are a high probability event. The best six months gives the Bear-o-Meter two positive points, making this part of the Bear-o-Meter a heavily weighted factor. The worst six months do not get a negative score — they get a neutral "0" rating.

DATE	40 WEEK A/D LINE	40 WEEK A/D LINE VS S&P 500 / CORRELATED =0	PE LEVEL / < 13 = 2	200 DAY MA	50 DAY MA	SMART/ DUMB SPREAD	INDU/TRAN	SEASONALITY	% ABOVE 50 DAY MA	VIX	PUT/CALL	NYHL	TOTAL
	>MA =1	BEARISH DIV. =-1	>23=0	>2	> =1	>0.25 =1	CORRELATED =0	Nov 1 – Apr 1 =2	<20=1	35=1	<0.75 =-1	<-200 =1	
	<MA =0	BULLISH DIV.=1	13<PE<23=1	<-2	< =0	<-0.25 =-1	DIVERGENCE =-1	May 1 – Oct 1 =0	>85=-1	12=-1	>1.25 =1	>300 =-1	

Figure 31: Bear-o-Meter Spreadsheet

Each of the above factors gets a score depending on their respective levels vs. historic buy/sell/neutral zones. I look for a total score to get a feel for risk and return potential. The Bear-o-Meter is assigned a scale of 0-8 total points based on the above. It can read over "8," but that's rare. In that almost-never-seen scenario, I still count the reading as "8." A reading of "0-3" is considered to have the potential for higher risk, while a reading of "5-8" is considered lower risk, higher reward potential. In between those levels is neutral. The diagram below is the one I put on my blog.

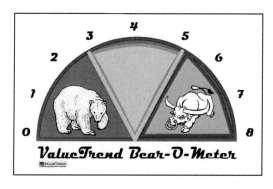

Figure 32: Bear-o-Meter Risk Gauge — Readings at or near "0" represent a higher risk environment on US stock markets. Readings at or near "8" represent a lower risk environment for US stock markets.

This tendency for the Bear-o-Meter to be a sometimes-long term leading indicator comes from the nature of its big picture indicators such as sentiment and breadth. Markets can remain "irrationally exuberant" or "excessively pessimistic" for long periods of time before they finally revert to their longer termed mean performance. The Bear-o-Meter is not designed to be a "buy/sell" system. I don't always get timely "low-risk" readings after a prior "high-risk" reading. I'm likely going to be early to exit, and late to re-enter if I try using the Bear-o-Meter for timing my entry and exits. So I tend to resort to incorporating traditional trend following buy/sell rules.

The Tale of Mary Contrarian

As I did in my first two books, *SmartBounce* and *Sideways*, I'll use a fictional character to illustrate the process in analyzing the markets using the three steps just discussed. Let's call our investor Mary Contrarian.

Mary has participated in every investment bubble since she began investing in the late 1990s. She bought into the hype that surrounded the technology bubble of the late 1990s by overloading her portfolio with technology stocks. After loosing her shirt in that experience, Mary swore she would never again be caught in an investment bubble.

The sub-prime mortgage/financial boom and commodity bubble in the years leading into 2008 saw Mary buying commodity stocks and bank stocks while chanting the mantras "oil to $200/barrel," and "They aren't making any more real estate." You'd think that the technology bubble of 2000 might have taught Mary a lesson on spotting irrational market exuberance. From her investment mistakes of the late 1990s, Mary should have learned how to spot the makings of an investment bubble. But, the influence of the crowd had inspired her to jump on some oil and gas income trusts and a host of financial institutions in the business of providing mortgage financing to the booming real estate sector. As markets declined aggressively in the 18 months following their 2007 peak, Mary watched her portfolio lose almost all of the progress she had made towards recovering from her 2001 investment mistakes.

The old adage "Once bitten, twice shy" has never applied to Mary's investment style. Since 2009, Mary has owned plenty of stocks, looking to profit through a compelling story of "the next big thing." She bought gold and oil in 2011 at market highs, before significant corrections. She jumped on the marijuana and Bitcoin bandwagon in 2018 with perfectly poor timing. In both cases, she sold in a panic near their bottoms after watching them fall from their lofty highs. It was time for a change.

Luckily, she happened upon the manuscript of *Smart Money, Dumb*

Money. After reading the book, Mary decided to apply the Three Steps to Portfolio Happiness before buying or selling any new securities in the future. Following the three-step approach outlined in *Smart Money, Dumb Money* has involved more time and effort than before. But, the results have been worth it. Mary feels comfortable with the returns and the risk controls that she has put into place since gaining a better understanding of contrarian investing. Let's turn the clock back to early 2017. We'll sit next to Mary with her newfound knowledge as she analyses the state of the markets. Let's watch as Mary decides her current investment moves as time rolled forward after 2017. We'll watch her employ her new, more disciplined investment strategy during both the good times and two severe market corrections.

January 2017

Using her trend-following tools discussed earlier in this chapter, Mary rode the bull market after the inauguration of Donald Trump in 2017. The market had been riding the wave of new business friendly policies and low interest rates brought on by the Trump administration. The S&P 500 had been making higher highs and lows on the weekly chart, while maintaining a healthy, but not overbought, distance above its 200 day (40 week) simple moving average. Since 2017 began, Bear-o-Meter readings had been consistently neutral or bullish. In early October of 2018, Mary noted one reading on her Bear-o-Meter score at the higher risk level of "1." However, the market was in an uptrend, and was only about 5% above its 200 day moving average. Based on that observation, she felt that if there was going to be a pullback, it wasn't likely to be too severe. She reduced her stock exposure by 15% that October as the S&P 500 approached 2900. Mary held the proceeds in cash.

The S&P 500 did fall a fairly severe 25% from September to December of 2018. Mary regretted not raising more cash than the 15% she had, but she consoled herself by acknowledging that the bigger trend indicators hadn't been showing major signs of deterioration. Technically, the market looked to be staging a "normal" correction. After its 2900 peak in September, the market had consolidated near its early 2018 trough support level near 2600. Despite the break of the 200 day moving average, the last low near 2600 had not been taken out on the chart. Mary decided to maintain her 15% cash weighting without raising further cash. Suddenly, the market fell hard and moved below its last low of 2600 on the weekly S&P 500 chart. There wasn't much she could have done to predict the extent of that December pullback after the consolidation in November. The break through 2600 had been fast and furious, leaving no time for Mary to raise further cash as the S&P 500 moved below 2400 on the index. But, at least she had raised that initial 15% cash. This helped to dampen her portfolios volatility, and provided capital to buy stocks at a cheaper price.

Thankfully, the December 2018 pullback didn't last too long. The markets immediately began to rally in early 2019. Mary followed her trading rules. She re-entered the market with her cash in March of 2019 only after the S&P 500 moved back over its 200-day moving average. The S&P 500 was back to 2700, meaning that it had taken out the last consolidation point on the chart. She noted that the Bear-o-Meter had maintained a bearish to neutral risk reading in January and February of 2019, but it had returned to bullish levels by March of that year. This coincided with her trend analysis, confirming her decision to deploy the cash and move back to fully invested status.

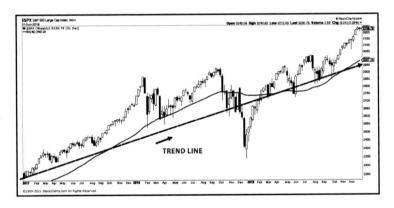

Figure 33: StockCharts — S&P 500 2017, 2020 With Trend Break In 2018. A trend break is defined by a lower low than the prior trough, and a break of the 200-day (40 week) simple moving average. Both conditions occurred December 2018. The trendline illustrates the uptrend.

Thankfully, the December 2018 pullback didn't last too long. The markets immediately began to rally in early 2019. Mary followed here trading rules. She re-entered the market with her cash in March of 2019 only after the S&P 500 moved back over its 200-day moving average. The S&P 500 was back to 2700, meaning that it had taken out the last consolidation point on the chart. She noted that the Bear-o-Meter had maintained a bearish to neutral risk reading in January and February of 2019, but it had returned to bullish levels by March of that year. This coincided with her trend analysis, confirming her decision to deploy the cash and move back to fully invested status.

Despite the fact that she was re-entering above the December lows, she was satisfied in knowing that she was still buying at market levels below where she had sold in October. More importantly, she had followed her strategy. She knew that she would have reduced her risk by continuing to raise cash, had the market maintained a declining trend and bearish profile.

Mary noted that the market was a little concentrated in technology stocks in early 2019, particularly the "FAANG" names (Facebook, Amazon, Apple, Netflix, Google). Still, the market was definably in an uptrend. Adding evidence to the strength of that uptrend, the Advance/Decline line illustrated positive breadth. Most of the near termed sentiment indicators were neutral, and the Bear-o-Meter continued to rank neutral to bullish over the summer of 2019.

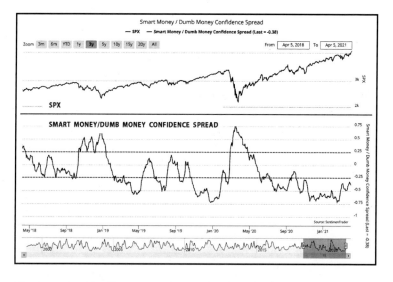

Figure 34: SentimenTrader — Smart Money/Dumb Money Confidence Spread. Note the spread was well below the "risk" line on the bottom of the chart between late 2019 and early 2020. It was clear that the market was irrationally exuberant in this timeframe, providing an ideal atmosphere for an amplified selloff when the COVID crash came.

As the year progressed, Mary noted that *Smart Money/Dumb Money* was becoming strained (too many bearish smart investors, too many bullish retail investors) in the second half of the year. She knew that this indicator is a very forward-looking risk assessment. Leading indicators like investor surveys can reach irrational crowd readings weeks to months ahead of major market movements.

Neutral readings on the volatility indicators like the VIX and the Put/Call ratio suggested that near termed investor sentiment wasn't too overdone. Most of the year illustrated fairly neutral signals on the Bear-o-Meter with no signs of technical trend deterioration. She remained fully invested during much of 2019, while remaining cognizant of the early warning signals she was getting from the *Smart Money/Dumb Money* Confidence Spread, shown in Figure 34, during the second half of the year.

February 2020

Something changed in early 2020. The S&P was trading about 10% over its 200-day moving average by February of that year. As discussed in chapter three under the subsection "Using moving averages to spot fear and greed," when the market moves much more than 10% over its 200-day moving average, this can be a sell signal. Mary recalled that when markets are about 15% ahead of the 200-day moving average, the odds for a correction could increase. The S&P 500 wasn't massively overbought, at 10% over its 200-day moving average, but it was now in that upper zone. She decided to keep an eye on that level. The Bear-o-Meter score was "3," at that same time. This is a neutral reading, but it was on the edge of a higher risk score for the market. Mary was growing nervous about the market's increasing risk profile.

She also noted the high-risk readings within the shorter termed sentiment indicators such as the high level of the CBOE Put/Call ratio (Figure 35). She noted the overbought readings on breadth indicators like the number of stocks that were above their 50-day moving averages as described earlier in this book (Figure 19). All factors taken into consideration, the only thing keeping her in the market was the overall trend on the weekly market chart, which was bullish, albeit somewhat overbought. Further, seasonality tended to be positive through the winter months, adding to the case for staying invested. Mary felt that, despite the bullish trend, the market was a little overbought based on its position over its 200-day moving average and the borderline Bear-o-Meter score of "3."

She began to reduce her stock holdings as the S&P reached 3400. She didn't want to fight the broader bullish trend too much, so she focused on selling only 10% of her more aggressively overbought positions. She held the proceeds as cash. She had noticed that some higher beta sectors such as technology, semi conductors and consumer discretionary stocks displayed particularly overbought technical momentum indicators like RSI and Stochastics (see my book *Sideways*).

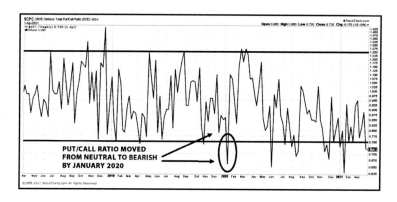

Figure 35: StockCharts — Put/Call Ratio. Note the transition into a higher risk market in January 2020 after many months of neutral risk, according to this indicator.

Mary, like most of us, didn't foresee the market crash that surrounded the world COVID crises in March of 2020. But she knew that markets were exhibiting some signs of near termed risk. Like her decision to raise cash in October of 2018 based on similar factors, her decision to raise 10% cash during February 2020's market exuberance allowed her to reduce some portfolio downside during the crash that followed. More importantly, through trend analysis and sentiment tools, Mary was able to identify when she could step back in with her cash to take advantage of new opportunities. By June of 2020, she was fully invested as the S&P 500 moved ahead of the old support point of 2800 and moved above its 200-day moving average after a brief retest of that line. Positive confirmation by her sentiment indicators suggested that the excessive readings seen in February had dissipated.

Once again, Mary had stuck with her discipline by reducing risk during an overbought market in February 2020. She managed to re-enter three months later in June of 2020 at a lower price, after her trend analysis

KEITH G. RICHARDS

rules (discussed earlier in this chapter) proved that a new bear market had not begun. As seen in Figure 35, the S&P 500 had moved through its 40-week moving average, followed by a successful test in June of 2020. This provided the technical trend evidence, which, combined with a neutral Bear-o-Meter reading, to go back to fully invested status.

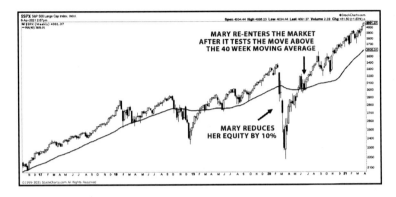

Figure 36: StockCharts — S&P 500 Illustrating Mary's February 2020 selling point & her June 2020 re-entry

Mary Contrarian is Quite CONTRARY!

Mary continues to exercise the discipline of trend-following and technical analysis techniques in her buy and sell decisions. Now, thanks to her interest in contrarian and sentiment indicators, she has a second discipline to refine her broader portfolio management decisions. When her contrarian indicators suggest risk is higher, she increases her cash holdings and reduces her individual security risk by selling higher beta stocks. When her contrarian indicators signal risk is lower, she has the confidence to re-enter the markets and buy higher beta positions. She does this, of course, only when the technical buy signals she gets from her charts confirm the signals from her sentiment indicators.

Mary is not a victim of her emotions. In fact, she now profits by the irrational crowd behaviour of other market participants. Mary follows John Templeton's original advice of "buying when others are despondently selling and selling when others are avidly buying."

To date, Mary has no tattoos, and does not drive a pickup truck …

Orther books by Keith Richards

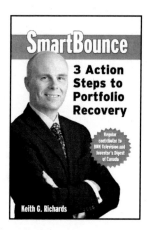

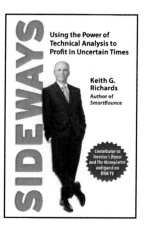

SmartBounce
3 Action Steps to Portfolio Recovery
ISBN 978-1-926645-68-1

MANY INVESTORS WATCHED IN HORROR as 30% or more of their portfolio vanished during the market massacre of 2008. If you are one of those investors, this book will teach you a better — and safer — way to invest. In SmartBounce Keith G. Richards describes three actions steps for recovering your portfolio:

- Choose the right time.
- Achieve the right balance.
- Be in the right place.

SIDEWAYS
Using the Power of Technical Analysis to Profit in Uncertain Times
Applicable to investors in all markets!
ISBN 978-1-926645-13-1

Today's sideways stock markets — markets that have hit both a floor and a ceiling — are likely to be with us until the middle of this decade or later. But you don't have to feel disoriented, according to Keith G. Richards. In his new book on investing, he shows you how to think and act like a technical analyst by understanding the basics of market realities — from phases to trends to formations and cycles. Sideways will help you profit from a financial reality that others are unsuccessfully fighting or fleeing.